PROFILES OF VALOR

Character Studies
from the
War of Independence

Marilyn Boyer &
Grace Tumas Ehrman

Master Books First Printing: November 2025

Master Books® is a division of the New Leaf Publishing Group, LLC.

ISBN: 978-1-68344-425-1
ISBN: 978-1-61458-944-0 (digital)

All Scripture verses are from the King James Version of the Bible.

Please consider requesting that a copy of this volume be purchased by your local library system.

Printed in the United States of America

Please visit our website for other great titles:
www.masterbooks.com

For information regarding promotional opportunities, please contact the publicity department at pr@nlpg.com.

Character Studies
from the
War of Independence

July 9, 1755 – June 17, 1775

Credits

Thanks to the following people for their investment in helping to preserve these inspiring stories from America's past. It is my prayer that their efforts will reap a bountiful harvest as these stories will serve to be an inspiration to those in whose hands America's future lies!

I wish to thank David Barton, who has been such an inspiration to me, personally, to become excited about learning about our godly heritage. God has gifted him for such a time as this in our country. He is the master of primary source documents! Tuesday night has traditionally been "Barton night" in our home as we gather to watch his presentations and invite friends in to learn with us! It is only as we get truth back into the public square that we can hope to preserve the heritage of freedom handed down to us.

Thanks to Grace Tumas Ehrman, for her role in crafting these stories in such a way that they are a delight to read! It's great when even the editors have to read the stories first to see what happens and then go back and edit!

Thanks to my dear friend Mary Ann Edman who is the world's most efficient multi-tasker, committed to producing quality that will be a tribute to our

Lord and Savior. Her creativity has been indispensable in producing the layout and graphic design for this book as well as editing the mistakes the rest of us overlooked!

Thanks to Judy Saunders, my long-time friend and prayer warrior, for her faithful work in the tedious editing process. God has gifted her with a precise eye for detail. She sees things I just don't notice. Thanks, my friend!

Thanks to my son, Rick, who, despite his incredibly busy life, has read these stories to his children at night, while editing each for accuracy of content to assure we are portraying these men and women in an worthy manner, giving honor where honor is due.

Chronological Table of Contents

Table of Contents by Character Quality

Introduction

In doing my research for *For You They Signed,* a book about the 56 signers of the Declaration of Independence, I discovered so many compelling stories that were about people other than the signers of the Declaration of Independence during this time of our history, that I felt I must share more of their stories with you.

It is crucial to understand the mindset of the founders who laid the foundations of the freedoms we enjoy today. We must understand that of course not everyone was a Christian, but what is true is that our government was based upon principles found in the Bible. Christianity shaped the very foundations by which our country was established.

When you read the founders' writings, you do not have to guess what they based their beliefs on. Many Christians today feel that the founders were in rebellion to seek their independence. This is far from the truth. Just read what they wrote and let them tell you where they got their ideas. A famous quote by James Madison proclaims that the future and success of America is not in the Constitution but in the laws of God upon which the Constitution was founded.

Samuel Adams, a signer of the Declaration of Independence, specifically recommended a study of the Scriptures to better understand the basis of America's struggle against a tyrannical king:

> *The Rights of the Colonists as Christians ... may be best understood by reading and carefully studying the institutes of the great Law Giver and Head of the Christian Church, which are to be found clearly written and promulgated in the New Testament.*[1]

The Rev. Dr. Jonathan Mayhew, a key preacher during the Great Awakening, in his famous 1750 sermon, coined the phrase, "Rebellion to tyrants is obedience to God." This idea that they were not rebelling against God or resisting ordained government, but only tyranny, was reflected in the fact that this phrase was suggested to be used for the first national motto in America, in August 1776.

It must be understood that the War of Independence was an act of self-defense, not an offensive war. England attacked the colonists. England fired the first shot at the Boston Massacre in 1770, at the bombing of Boston and burning of Charlestown in 1774, and during the attacks on Williamsburg, Concord, and Lexington in 1775. The command to the Lexington Minutemen, "Don't fire unless fired upon!" was the standard set by the colonists. They did, however, believe in the right to self-defense.

This attitude is reflected in the appeal made by Stephen Hopkins (a signer of the Declaration) when he explained to the British:

> *We finally beg leave to assert that the first planters of these colonies were pious Christians—were faithful [British] subjects who, with a fortitude and perseverance little known and less considered, settled these wild countries by God's goodness and their own amazing labors [and] thereby added a most valuable dependence to the crown of Great Britain; were ever dutifully subservient to her interests; so taught their children that not one has been disaffected to this day but all have honestly obeyed every royal command and cheerfully submitted to every constitutional law; ... have carefully avoided every offensive measure ... have never been troublesome or expensive to the mother country; have kept due order and supported a regular government; have maintained peace and practiced Christianity; and in all conditions and in every relation have demeaned themselves as loyal, as dutiful, and as faithful subjects ought; and that no kingdom or state hath, or ever had, colonies more quiet, more obedient, or more profitable than these have ever been.*[2]

Their many appeals were met with disdain from King George, although there were men in Parliament that sided with the colonies.

Freedom is fragile. Vigilance must be constantly practiced to ensure that our freedoms are not confiscated from our very midst. The first sign of a society's decay is when their history is taken from them. We, of all nations, have a godly heritage, and we are responsible for uncovering it and teaching it to our children. Our freedom was bought at an enormous price by so many. It is my prayer that as you learn of our forgotten heritage, you will be inspired to pick up the torch and protect our fast-disappearing freedoms with your last ounce of courage. Learn from the lives of those who have gone before you and, inspired by their sacrifice, persevere with all boldness to leave a legacy of freedom to those who come behind us.

Marilyn Boyer

...every man living in or out of a state of civil society has a right peaceably and quietly to worship God according to the dictates of his conscience.

—Samuel Adams, The Rights of the Colonists

Humility

DEFINITION

Acknowledging that any good
I have achieved is a gift from God,
and my life is to be used as an
instrument in His hand

MEMORY VERSE

And whosoever shall exalt
himself shall be abased;
and he that shall humble himself
shall be exalted.
Matthew 23:12

Bulletproof Coat

Col. George Washington

Monongahela, Pennsylvania
July 9, 1755

That year the French Canadians crept closer to the American border, intent on seizing the rich lands in the Ohio River Valley. They began sending their Algonquin and Iroquois allies into Virginia to attack and burn frontier settlements. After scalping and taking prisoners, the tribes disappeared over the mountains to the safety of French Fort Duquesne on the Monongahela River. Virginia's Governor Robert Dinwiddie realized that the European conflict with France, the "Seven Years'

War," had turned into a small world war. During the past few years, the British and French traded the colonies back and forth, shifting borders with Canada and signing peace treaties that usually lasted only a short time. Now Dinwiddie had a battle for the Ohio Valley on his hands. Which country controlled the area depended on who arrived first, gained Native American allies, built forts, and began ferrying new settlers over the mountains.

Dinwiddie had instructions from the British government to prevent the French from establishing forts at all costs. Quickly, the governor organized two small expeditions, one led by British General Edward Braddock. A twenty-two-year-old colonel

Tribes fighting the colonists

The retreat of General Braddock

named George Washington commanded the other. Plunging into the Monongahela wilderness in Pennsylvania, French and British forces collided in a skirmish. During the confusion, a French officer, possibly an emissary, was killed. The French immediately called for revenge. As they dug in at their stronghold at Fort Duquesne, Braddock decided to march against them with thirteen hundred troops.

By this time, the colonists had dubbed the conflict on the frontier the French and Indian War, instead of the Seven Years' War in faraway Europe. It demonstrated their growing sense of national identity and their preoccupation with affairs on the home front. Braddock and his British Regulars and a number of "Continentals" or colonists set off to confront the French. On the way, Washington took Braddock aside and tried to dissuade him from marching into a forest full of French and Native Americans as if he were on a parade ground, back in London.

Braddock snapped: "[They] may frighten Continental troops, but they can make no impression on the King's Regulars!"

The British looked down on the colonists as rough country bumpkins, while the colonists viewed their British officers as aristocratic snobs. A high percentage of British officers had bought their commissions, meaning that many of them had little practical military experience. The militiamen, on the other hand, had not received much army training. The frontiersmen dressed in rugged homespun clothes suitable for the terrain, while British officers struggled through tall grass, deep rivers and along narrow forest paths in white gaiters and long, tightly-buttoned crimson coats with a crescent-shaped brass gorget nestling at the throat. They disagreed over fighting techniques as well. General Braddock believed that his soldiers ought to advance in neat block ranks according to form, keeping in step and facing the enemy at all times. But Washington, leading a band of frontiersmen, knew better. Since the Native Americans fought darting from tree to tree, his men fought that way also. It was the only way to survive in the wilderness.

Portrait of Colonel George Washington

Washington's worst fears came true all too soon. Seven miles from Fort Duquesne, the enemies ambushed the party. They opened shattering gunfire from behind boulders, trees, and thickets. The British regulars wheeled as they were taught, stood shoulder to shoulder out in the open and went down like ninepins. Braddock fell with a shot through his chest. Within minutes, eighty-five officers had been killed or wounded. Seven hundred fourteen soldiers lay dead on the ground or crawled away into the forest. That day, the tribes claimed, the white man's blood mixed with the streams of the forest.

Suddenly, an Algonquin chief caught sight of George Washington rallying his frontiersmen on horseback. Turning to one of his young men, the chief exclaimed: "Mark tall and daring warrior. He is not of the red coat tribe. He hath...wisdom, and his warriors fight as we do. See him alone—exposed. Quick, let your aim be certain so he dies."

Instantly the Algonquins silently leveled their rifles. Their black eyes squinted as they sighted along the barrel, aiming at the tall man's chest. Their muskets cracked, filling the woods with murky grey powder smoke. Bullets pinged through the air. Washington heard a buzz like a bee, and a bullet sliced through his coat. He rode on. Bullets splattered against tree trunks, horses whinnied and plunged. The Algonquian chief kept telling his men to fire at Washington. A second and then a third bullet pierced his uniform. Suddenly, his horse shuddered and sank to the ground. Washington rolled out from under the horse as it went down heavily. Jumping to his feet, he seized a rider-less horse as it dashed by. A fourth bullet ripped through his coat, but again it had not touched him. Another horse stumbled and fell. There was no time to think, no time to act except by instinct. But at that moment, Washington felt that an "all-powerful dispensation of Providence" was protecting him "beyond all human probability or expectation."

Suddenly the Algonquian chief shouted: "Stop firing!"

Beside him, another muttered: "I had seventeen clear shots at him and after all could not bring him to the ground. This man was not born to be killed by a bullet."

Swinging tomahawks, they leaped upon the dead and wounded, carrying off scalps as trophies. They took no prisoners. Washington, the only officer left on horseback, managed to rally the scattered British and Continental soldiers and led them back across the Monongahela River to safety.

Fifteen years later, Washington and his family physician, Dr. James Craik, passed near the joining of the Kanawha and Ohio rivers. All at once, a group of Native Americans led by an ancient Algonquian chief approached them. Sitting down, the chief stared at Washington across the flames of a council fire. Speaking through an interpreter, the chief went back to that July day in 1755. He told Washington how his men, who never missed, had shot at the young colonel again and again.

"'Twas all in vain." His voice rose. "A Power, mightier far than we, gave him protection from bullets. He cannot die in battle. I am old and soon shall be gathered to the Great Council of Fire of my fathers in the Land of Shades, but ere I go, there is something bids me speak in voice of Great Spirit. Listen! The Great Spirit protects this warrior Washington and will guide his path. He will become the chief of great nations and of many people, yet unborn. People will say of him, he like me, [is] Chief of a mighty nation!"

Several years after the battle, Samuel Davies, a "New Light" Presbyterian minister in Hanover, Virginia, spoke of Washington's escape. "I cannot but hope," he said, that "Providence has hitherto preserved him in so singular a manner for some important service to his country."

When Washington accepted command of the Continental Army during the Revolution, it became clear that he had been preserved for this purpose twenty years before. Washington never doubted that God had saved his life that day. He demonstrated humility by taking no credit for the bulletproof coat. But the influx of British troops to the colonies due to the French and Indian War would have a direct effect on America's future. Tensions surfaced between the British Regulars and the militiamen during the conflict. These tensions demonstrated how far the colonies and Great Britain had drifted apart. The British sent more troops to the colonies in order to strengthen them against Native American attacks over the next two decades, but this only served to increase suspicion and tensions among the colonists who believed that the British were trying to turn the colonies into a military state.

When the Revolutionary War ended in 1783, George III learned that Washington had turned in his resignation rather than seize power as a king or dictator. Amazed at the humility that Washington demonstrated, King George exclaimed: "If he does that, he'll prove to be the greatest man in the world."

This nation, and the other nations of Europe, may thereby learn, with more certainty, the grounds of a dissension that possibly may, sooner or later, have consequences interesting to them all.

—Benjamin Franklin,
Preface to the English
Edition of the Report
of the Committee of
Correspondence

Questions

1. What is the definition of humility? How did Colonel Washington's life reflect humility?
2. How do we know God protected George Washington's life?
3. Tell the account of Washington's "bulletproof" coat.
4. What was the conclusion the Algonquin chief drew concerning George Washington?
5. To what did George Washington attribute the preservation of his life during the ambush near Fort Duquesne?
6. How many times did one Native American claim to have shot at Washington?
7. What did Samuel Davies say of Washington?
8. King George's pronouncement of Washington's character perhaps speaks conclusively of his humility. What did King George say?
9. God has a special purpose for your life. Your life is in God's hand, just as Washington's was. To whom should you attribute any good you may accomplish?

Enthusiasm

DEFINITION

Expressing joy in each job
I am given to do

MEMORY VERSE

Rejoice in the Lord alway:
and again I say, Rejoice.
Philippians 4:4

Father of Civil Liberty

Rev. Jonathan Mayhew

Boston, Massachusetts
June 8, 1766

He looked up from his knees as light streamed suddenly into the room. Somehow, the night had passed and Sunday morning arrived while he wrestled through issues facing the American colonies. Forty-six-year-old Jonathan Mayhew, orator and Harvard graduate, had already made waves as a minister at West Church in Boston, Massachusetts. Now, as he grappled with the tyranny of the Stamp Act and British legislation that increasingly hobbled the colonies' liberties, Mayhew knew that he needed

Reverend Jonathan Mayhew

answers. Separated by distance and the difficulties of communication, the Northern, Southern, and Middle colonies had no way to distribute information or organize resistance to the acts of the British Parliament. They needed a system that could rapidly inform each other of hostile developments, create militias, and unify their beliefs.

Writing to his close friends John Hancock, John Adams, Samuel Adams, the fiery lawyer James Otis, James Bowdoin, and Thomas Paine, the young minister actively swayed these men towards independence. His sermons regularly circulated throughout the country. They were read, digested, discussed. In the past sixteen years, Mayhew had become the greatest clerical proponent of civil and religious liberty in America.

He remembered preaching a white-hot sermon at West Church on a cold January day in 1750. Titled "A Discourse Concerning Unlimited Submission and Non-resistance to the Higher Powers," Mayhew's words ripped through the congregation, setting it on fire. Staring up at the famous preacher sat an eager, fifteen-year-old boy named Paul Revere. He would never forget the patriot minister's flaming words about the tyranny of Britain and the rights of Englishmen to throw off an oppressive government. The people must resist tyranny, Mayhew argued, even to the point of "chopping off of kings' heads," a reference to the execution of Charles I in 1649. Circulated by horseback throughout the colonies and Great Britain, Mayhew's sermon, according to John Adams, "fired the opening gun of the Revolution." Patriot, orator, scholar, reformer, and incisive writer, Mayhew became the first clergyman to preach active resistance to the British.

Now, as he rose from his knees, sunlight streamed through the windows. The year before, Mayhew, incensed by the 1765 Stamp Act, argued that slavery was basically subjection to others, "whether many, few, or but one, it matters not."

Dawn broke as light flooded his mind that Sunday morning. Suddenly, he knew what to do. Reaching for a sheet of paper, Mayhew dipped his quill in ink and began his last letter to James Otis. "You have heard of the communion of the churches; while I was thinking of this ... [the] importance of the colonies appeared to me in a striking light. Would it not be decorous in our Assembly to send circulars to all the rest [of the colonies] expressing a desire to cement a union among ourselves? ... It may be the only means of perpetuating our liberties." With a passionate flourish, he concluded: "Communion of churches! Why not communion of the colonies?"

He had created a direct link between Protestant Christianity and the concept of revolution. The Committees of Correspondence, first suggested by Jonathan Mayhew, later proved vital in protecting the colonists' freedom, spreading news, serving as spy networks, and organizing militia units. The first public expression of a more perfect union, created for the common defense of the people and the future glory of the United States, originated in the mind of Jonathan Mayhew. He would die a month later of a "nervous fever" contracted while riding home on horseback in wet weather from a minister's conference.

His friend James Otis called Mayhew "a master-workman, Christ-like, who broke down the partition wall between secular and religious affairs." John Adams also placed Mayhew on a par with Samuel Adams and James Otis as a patriot-statesman.

"To draw the character of Mayhew," Adams wrote, "would be to transcribe a dozen volumes." Today, Jonathan Mayhew is known as the "Father of Civil Liberty."

Jonathan Mayhew's practical enthusiasm in his appeal for freedom helped to define the cause of religious and civil liberty which was critical to understanding the motivations behind the Declaration of Independence and the U.S. Constitution. His philosophies and arguments not only deeply influenced the Founding Fathers, but helped to shape the language with which they defined the rights of Englishmen, the right to overthrow a tyrannical government, and the concept of a unified nation.

All civil rulers, as such, are the ordinance and ministers of God; and they are all, by the nature of their office, and in their respective spheres and stations, bound to consult the public welfare.

—Jonathan Mayhew

Questions

1. How was Jonathan Mayhew's enthusiasm used like a spark to ignite patriotism?
2. What idea did Reverend Mayhew design to help keep the colonies connected with each other? Where did he get this idea?
3. By what means did his enthusiasm spread to others throughout the colonies?
4. From where did Reverend Mayhew develop his ideas about resistance to tyranny?
5. What did John Adams say fired the opening gun of the Revolution?
6. What did the Committee of Correspondence accomplish?
7. What did James Otis say of Jonathan Mayhew?
8. How can you use enthusiasm to inspire those around you?

Passion

DEFINITION

Expressing a compelling emotion toward a worthy cause, zealous

MEMORY VERSE

But it is good to be zealously
affected always in a good thing,
and not only when
I am present with you.
Galatians 4:18

Son of Liberty

Samuel Adams

Boston, Massachusetts
March 5, 1770

He was called "The Firebrand of the Revolution." A key leader of the Sons of Liberty, Sam Adams worked tirelessly, first to persuade the British government to grant the American colonists the full rights of Englishmen, and when that failed, to secure the independence of the thirteen colonies and their establishment as independent states.

Adams' fiery rhetoric had a mesmerizing effect on his hearers, often moving them to acts of daring and self-denial that seem amazing to modern readers. Yet his passion for justice and freedom were always seasoned with a deep reverence for God and a love for his fellow man. His deeply-held faith in Christ influenced all aspects of his life. Inspired by Scripture and his strong sense of honor, he placed his own personal comforts secondary to the beloved cause of freedom. He believed with all his heart that God was author of liberty, and he strove to be used as an instrument in God's hand.

During the dark days of September 1777, he encouraged others by proclaiming, "numerous have been the manifestations of God's providence in sustaining us. In the gloomy period of adversity, we have had 'our cloud by day and pillar of fire by night.'"

On another occasion, he declared, "The name of our Lord (says the Scripture) is a strong tower; thither the righteous flee and are safe (Proverbs 18:10). Let us secure His favor and He will lead us through the journey of this life and at length receive us to a better."

As much as Sam Adams objected to the unconstitutional acts of the British government, he was not in favor of violent resistance as long as there remained any hope of peaceful solutions. He favored organized and systematic opposition against the unwarranted encroachments of the crown, but not war. Yet when war came, Samuel Adams was a part of the fuse that ignited the explosion.

"The Boston Massacre," engraving by Paul Revere

He was instrumental in establishing the Committees of Correspondence and the Continental Congress that assembled at Philadelphia in 1774. He corresponded with the eminent patriots of the middle and southern states and contributed largely in producing unity of sentiment and concert of action in the glorious cause of liberty throughout the colonies.

When the Boston Massacre occurred on the 5th of March, 1770, between the British soldiers and a noisy group of citizens, the influence of Samuel

Adams prevented further bloodshed. Many of the colonists had become roused and were on the point of avenging the death of their friends who had just fallen. Mr. Adams shouted for the attention of the assembled mob and proposed peaceful measures to resolve the situation.

Mr. Adams was one day surprised by a message from British Governor Gage offering him a bribe to renounce his objections to English policy. It was made plain that if he refused he would be arrested and sent to England, there to be tried for high treason. The punishment was death.

Mr. Adams rose from his chair and said, "I trust I have long since made my peace with the King of Kings. No personal consideration shall induce me to abandon the righteous cause of my country."

This reply enraged the governor and when he later issued a proclamation offering a free pardon to those "rebels" who would return to what he termed their duty, he made exceptions in the case of Samuel Adams and John Hancock—the highest compliment within his power to bestow on the two patriots.

No bribe could move Mr. Adams from the path of duty and no threat could divert him. He placed his trust in the Rock of Ages—enjoyed the unlimited confidence of his friends, the approval of every patriot. These were more important to him than all the honors offered or threats made by earthly rulers.

Sam Adams, along with his friend John Hancock, became a special object of vengeance to the British.

Reverend Jonas Clark's house, Lexington, Massachusetts

It was because the two patriots were staying at the home of Reverend Jonas Clark at Lexington that the redcoated troops stopped there on their way to seize patriot weapons and supplies stored at nearby Concord on April 19, 1775. Finding out what the British intended to do, General Joseph Warren sent a rider to the two patriots warning them of approaching danger. Adams and Hancock escaped ahead of the British, but just a few hours later the "shot heard round the world" was heard on Lexington Common.

The war had begun.

Mr. Adams remained in the neighborhood during the night. The next morning, as the sun rose without an intervening cloud, he remarked to a friend, "This is a glorious day for America." He viewed the sacrifice of American blood at Lexington as a down payment on the freedom of future generations.

Samuel Adams

To rouse the people to action now became the sole business of this devoted friend of his bleeding country. The grand signal for action had been given—the war cry had been sounded and it was responded to by millions of patriotic hearts.

Mr. Adams mourned deeply the death of his friends but he believed their blood would cry to Heaven for vengeance and incite the hardy sons of America's soil to vigorous and triumphant action. The event added new strength to his persuasive powers and doubly nerved him to meet the fiery trials in reserve for him. As dangers increased he became more urgent for the people to maintain their rights. As the wrath of his enemies waxed hotter he was more highly appreciated by the people and he became known as Samuel Adams the Patriot. His fame and influence strengthened under persecution, his friends were inspired by his words, his foes were astounded and frustrated at the boldness of his onward career.

In the Congress of 1776 he was among the first to advocate the Declaration of Independence—contending that it should have followed immediately after the battle of Lexington. When the Declaration of Rights was adopted he signed his name to it, though he knew it meant the condemnation of the king.

During the darkest periods of the Revolution he was calm and cheerful and did much to encourage his fellow patriots. In 1777 when Congress was obliged to flee Philadelphia before the approach of the British army and a dismal gloom hung over the cause of the patriots, some members of Congress were in company with Mr. Adams lamenting recent military setbacks, concluding that the chances for success were very small. Mr. Adams promptly replied, “If this be our language, they are so indeed. If we wear long faces they will become fashionable. Let us banish such feelings and show a spirit that will keep alive the confidence of the people. Better tidings will soon arrive. Our cause is just and righteous. We shall never be abandoned by Heaven while we show ourselves worthy of its aid and protection.”

Not only through his life but even after his death, the reason for the faith, dedication, and passion of Sam Adams was obvious. In his Last Will and Testament he declared, “I ... rely upon the merits of Jesus Christ for a pardon for all my sins.”

I rely on the merits of Jesus Christ
as a pardon for all my sins.

—Samuel Adams

Questions

1. For what cause did Sam Adams work tirelessly? What was he called?
2. How did Adams' love for Christ and the Scriptures influence his passion for freedom?
3. What did he see as his role?
4. How did he use his passion to encourage others during the dark days of the conflict?
5. What was Sam Adams' position on the use of violence to obtain freedom?
6. What was he instrumental in organizing?
7. How did Sam Adams' influence prevent bloodshed during the Boston Massacre?
8. Tell about the bribe Governor Gage offered him and his response to it as well.
9. Why were Sam Adams and John Hancock especially hunted by the British?
10. Where were these two patriots as the British were marching toward Lexington? How did they escape?
11. What did Mr. Adams proclaim the next morning?

12. Who was the first person to advocate the Declaration of Independence?
13. How did he encourage others by pointing them to the Word of God?
14. Tell Sam Adams' words that testify of his belief in Jesus Christ.
15. Passion can be used rightly and wrongly. Tell of some of your passions that can be used for good. How can you influence others to do the right thing?

Justice

DEFINITION

Taking personal responsibility to uphold what is pure, right, and true

MEMORY VERSE

Blessed are they that
keep judgment,
and he that doeth
righteousness at all times.
Psalm 106:3

Justice Reigns

John Adams

Boston, Massachusetts

March 5, 1770

Church bells pealing loudly pulled John Adams from the Green Dragon Tavern in the South End Street, where he often met with the Sons of Liberty. Bells ringing meant fire. The thirty-five-year-old Boston lawyer stepped out into the frosty night air. Peering in the direction of the madly-ringing bells, he saw that the cobblestone street stretched blank and silver in the moonlight. Like his friends, Paul Revere and Samuel Adams, both local fire-wardens, Adams considered firefighting a community effort in a town full of combustible wooden buildings. He pushed his way into the street, joining a surging crowd of people. Borne along on the tide, Adams found himself swept towards King Street. There, he found a startling sight: a thin line of British soldiers stood facing a stretch of bloodstained ice. Five townspeople lay dead or dying in the snow.

It had all happened so suddenly. One moment, Adams had been chatting calmly and cheerfully with his fellow patriots. His pregnant wife, Abigail was home with his three-year-old son, John Quincy Adams, waiting up for him. She would be frightened if she heard the alarm bells ringing in the night. He hurried home to reassure her. Passing through the lonely streets on his way home, Adams saw little groups of British soldiers, standing frozen in formation, with shouldered muskets and fixed bayonets, as still as "marble statues."

Adams had just witnessed the aftermath of the "Boston Massacre." He still did not know what had actually happened. He also did not realize that he would soon be embroiled in one of the most controversial cases of his life.

The roots of the "massacre" began earlier that week with a seemingly insignificant tussle between a British soldier and some dockworkers. Tensions were high in Boston. The British, who were supposed to be their own countrymen, were occupying their city—sleeping in their houses and in some cases, eating their food. Armed guards were enforcing curfews and unreasonable tariffs and regulations. It was unthinkable that their rights as Englishmen were being trampled on. They had appealed to King George, only to have more regulations and taxes forced upon them. They were watching as their freedoms were in danger of disintegrating.

Depiction of the Boston Massacre showing Crispus Attucks

On Friday, March 2, an off-duty British soldier hesitated near a group of Boston rope-makers and asked if they had any work. The British army paid their soldiers paltry wages, and they often tried to do odd jobs around Boston in exchange for a bit of pocket money. "Do you have any work?" the solider asked. One of the rope-makers spoke up. "You can go clean my outhouse," he answered.

Aftermath of the massacre: five dead, three wounded

The British soldier was highly offended. Someone threw a punch, and a fight broke out. The soldier managed to tear himself away and ran off, returning a few minutes later with several of his friends. A small brawl erupted. One of the soldiers, Matthew Killroy and one of the rope-makers,

Governor Thomas Hutchinson

Samuel Grey, would meet again soon under much bloodier circumstances.

Three days later, on the evening of Monday, March 5, a lone British sentry stood on guard outside the Boston Customs House on King Street, in order to protect the import duties collected for King George III. Around 8 p.m., a barber's apprentice named Edward Garrick ran up and requested payment for a job he'd completed for the British soldier. The soldier refused to pay. A fight broke out, and the soldier swung his musket, hitting the boy on the head. Soon a crowd began to gather, and another British soldier named Hugh Montgomery dared them to fight.

Within minutes, a gang of twenty-five sailors and dockworkers came round the corner, screaming, whistling, and carrying heavy wooden clubs.

A symbol of the Sons of Liberty

"Bloody lobster back!" they shouted. Crispus Attucks, a tall, stocky sailor, half-Native American, half-African, shoved his way to the front. He held a raised cudgel in his hand. The group swelled in number to about one hundred people, and a few angry Bostonians threw icy snowballs at the sentry. Alarmed, the sentry loaded his musket. The frightened sentry began to call for help. Hugh Montgomery, the only other British soldier nearby, ran off towards the nearest barracks. He pounded on the door, yelling: "Turn out, Main Guard!"

Forty-year-old Captain Thomas Preston had drawn duty for officer of the day on March 5 when one of his soldiers alerted him to the dangerous situation on King Street. Not a hothead by any means, Preston began pacing in front of the Main Guard in the barracks. Lt. Colonel Carr, Preston's commanding officer, called him "as cool and distinct as any officer of his rank and service." At the same time, Preston's options were slim. He understood the hatred leveled at him and his men as British soldiers. At the same time, he could not let two of his men possibly get attacked by an angry crowd. Finally, after pacing for half an hour, Preston made up his mind. "Turn out!" he yelled to his 29th Regiment. Buttoning his red coat and clamping his lace tricorn hat on his head, Preston drew his sword and marched at the head of his eight-man squad towards the uproar on King Street.

He ordered his men, six privates and a corporal, into a semi-circle in front of the Customs House. Preston took up his place a little ways behind them. The surging crowd, pushed against the thin line of soldiers, some calling out: "Lobsters! Bloody backs!" Crispus Attucks and some others in the crowd beat at the soldiers' muskets with sticks and clubs.

Suddenly, a club struck Hugh Montgomery in the chest, knocking him painfully to the ice. "Fire," someone hollered. Furious, the soldier struggled to his feet, squeezed the trigger and fired. Beside

Samuel Adams

him, Private Matthew Killroy fired as well. One of their bullets hit the rope-maker, Samuel Grey, the dockworker who beat up Killroy three days before. As the soldiers loaded for a second round, Preston shouted: "Stop firing! Do not fire!" Five men lay on the reddened snow. In the first shock, nobody believed that the bodies were real.

Word of the shooting reached Governor Thomas Hutchinson at his home in North Square. Rushing towards King Street, the governor met a raging crowd howling for blood. Horrified, he jerked Captain Preston aside. "Do you know, sir," he snapped, "you have no power to fire on anybody of the public collected together except you have a civil magistrate with you to give orders?" Preston protested that he had not ordered the shooting. Amid the chaos, the captain gathered his men and marched them back to the garrison. Hutchinson turned and scurried up the stairs to the Town House. There, he called an emergency meeting with several town council members to address the situation. As a crowd gathered below, Hutchinson stepped out onto the balcony overlooking the bloody snow and called for quiet. "Let the law have its course," he declared. "I will live and die by the law."

Captain Preston was arrested sometime after midnight. Brought under guard to the Town House, the British officer spent most of the night undergoing an interrogation by two justices. Finally, at three in the morning, the guards hustled him to the jail and threw him into a cell. He would remain there for the next seven months. From jail, Preston dashed off pathetic letters to the *Boston Gazette*, thanking those in town who decided to defend an innocent British army captain in spite of the popular hatred. As he continued to sit in prison, however, Preston's tone grew bitter. He felt that the Bostonians had tried to break up his beloved regiment during this affair, making them more despised by encouraging desertions and inventing lies about them.

The next day, Sam Adams and the Sons of Liberty gathered at Faneuil Hall to demand the removal of all British troops from Boston. When Hutchinson protested that he had no authority to do so, Adams threatened that nothing short of complete military evacuation would preserve the peace. Hutchinson turned pale. Later that same month, two British regiments marched out of Boston and sailed for Castle William in the Boston Harbor.

Both Patriots and loyalists published pamphlet accounts with wildly different stories. Henry Pelham, the half-brother of artist John Singleton Copley, sketched out the first picture of the "massacre." Paul Revere, putting his engraving talents to use, picked up the image and copied it.

Sam Adams kept busy in the meantime, helping James Bowdoin write *A Short Narrative of the Horrid Massacre in Boston.* The Sons of Liberty published an account of the confrontation that left five dead and three wounded. Artists colored and distributed prints of the engraving showing Crispus Attucks dying on the ground. In farmhouses across New England, colonists cut out Revere's engraving, showing the "lobster backs" and bleeding victims, from the pages of the Boston Gazette and hung them prominently in their homes.

Many Bostonians wanted the captain and his men hung immediately or sent to stand trial. Although Governor Hutchinson managed to postpone the trial till autumn, Preston, as an Irish officer and a

Robert Treat Paine

Catholic, found himself in a bad situation. No one would defend him. Finally, a Tory merchant named Forrester sought out Boston lawyer John Adams begging him to take the case.

Despite the extreme unpopularity of such an action, Adams agreed. "I had no hesitation in answering that Counsel ought to be the very last thing that an accused Person should want in a free Country," he exclaimed. Although a patriot, Adams believed firmly that the British captain and his men deserved a fair, legal trial. He worried about the future of self-government in the colonies if the people were not given a fair representation. Preston only wanted the public to know the facts and for the law to take its due course. He couldn't afford to pay Adams more than a single guinea.

On September 8, Attorney General Jonathan Sewall drew up the indictment, although he did not believe these citizen-soldiers guilty. It read: "not having the fear of God before their eyes, but being moved and seduced by the Instigation of the devil and their own wicked Hearts," committed murder "against the peace of the said Lord the King, his Crown and Dignity."

The court selected a jury and appointed the defenders and prosecutors, including Robert Treat Paine. Samuel Quincy, one of John Adams' Harvard schoolmates, stood to prosecute Captain Preston, but a conviction would require a unanimous vote.

Even with Adams working for his defense, Preston had little hope of being acquitted. The captain faced four grim-faced judges. They wore the red robes that signified a death-penalty case. The court sat to determine one question: did Captain Preston order his men to fire on the mob? Although Preston denied this, the judges did not let him testify on his own behalf. After listening to conflicting testimony from dozens of witnesses all day on October 24, the jury adjourned to the jail-keeper's house nearby. The jury, prohibited from seeing outsiders until they had decided on a verdict, enjoyed a meal, before they returned back to court to hear a second round of testimony.

On the second day, Captain Preston had to listen to the most dangerous testimony yet. "I looked the officer in the face when he gave the word and saw his mouth," swore the prosecutor's witness. "…I saw his face plain, the moon shone on it. I am sure of the man though I have not seen him since before yesterday when he came into Court with others. I knew him instantly." Another witness declared under oath that a civilian had struck the captain, causing Preston to draw his sword and shout: "Fire! Think I'll be treated in this manner?" When the soldiers fired their first round, this man swore, Preston ordered a second volley. Despite such damaging statements, most of the witnesses insisted that

Preston had not ordered his men to fire.

Preston stated in his deposition that he genuinely believed that if he had not ordered his troops out to the rescue, the Boston mob would have murdered his sentry that night. He also feared that the crowd intended to rob the King's chest at the Custom's House nearby. On the morning of the fourth day, Saturday, October 27, Adams rose to give the first of the defense's closing arguments. After a week of debate, the jury found Captain Preston not guilty.

Sam Adams and other Sons of Liberty were upset at his acquittal, but they knew that he had never been accused of shooting at the crowd himself. Most Bostonians, including Sam Adams were not in favor of violence to obtain freedom. The sentiment was much like the order given at the Battle of Lexington, "Don't fire unless fired upon." Nevertheless, they demanded that someone should pay for the five men who had died.

The soldiers' trial began on November 27, with a different jury than had tried Captain Preston, but with the same four judges. John Hodgson, a shorthand writer, sat in the courtroom, scribbling a transcript of the trial. John Adams, along with Samson Blowers and Josiah Quincy, stood for the defense. Adams had hired private investigators to check around town to collect evidence. The trial lasted a full week with over eighty witnesses testifying.

Turning to the jury, Adams opened his argument

with the claim that it was better for a guilty man to escape than for an innocent one to be punished. He

John Adams

made the jury see the screaming crowd, making sounds "almost as terrible as ... [a] yell," and argued that the men had fired out of sheer self-defense.

The prosecution, on the other hand, alleged that after months of continuous contempt by the townspeople, all the soldiers went out to King's Street that day with murder in their hearts. Against this onslaught, John Adams, on the defense team, had to overcome some serious obstacles. If Preston did not order his men to fire, then why did they fire without a command? Adams demonstrated that the crowd had endangered the soldiers. They had to convince a strong, anti-British jury of this. So they concentrated on the actions of the mob that threatened the captain and his men. Witnesses spoke of verbal taunts, curses, threats, and insults that escalated into violence as the mob struck soldiers with objects ranging from snowballs and chunks of coal, to sticks and cudgels. Dr. John Jefferies stated that even the victim Patrick Carr, who died ten days after the attack, insisted on his deathbed that he felt the soldiers had fired simply in self defense. He did not blame the man who shot him. Skillfully, John Adams focused his closing argument on educating the jury on the principles of self-defense. He brought before their minds the vivid scene of the angry crowd roaring: "Kill them! Knock them over!" John Adams asked each of the jurors to picture themselves in those soldiers' shoes on that cold March night. Then he demanded, "Judge whether a reasonable man ... would not have concluded they were going to kill him."

Despite his patriot sympathies, Adams painted an unappealing picture of the crowd as "a motley rabble of saucy boys ..." He begged the jury to set aside their prejudices for the moment and consider the case as if the soldiers were not British, but merely men. Finally, Adams pointed them back to the law. "If an assault was made to endanger their lives, the law is clear, they had the right to kill in self-defense." Adams agreed that if the attack "was not so severe as to endanger their lives [then] this was a provocation, for which the law reduces the offense of killing down to manslaughter." In either case, the men should not hang.

Paine, concluding the case for the prosecution, insisted that the soldiers had "unlawfully" assembled in front of the Customs House, loaded their muskets with double shot, and thereby angered the crowd. Then they simply opened fire out of pure malice. Finally, Paine called on the jurors to find all eight soldiers guilty of first-degree murder. After two and a half hours' deliberation, the jury acquitted six of the soldiers. In the case of Montgomery and Killroy, the jury decided that even though they felt threatened by the crowd, they should have held their fire instead of firing directly into it. The jury found both guilty of manslaughter, but the men pleaded the "privilege of clergy," a procedure that reduced punishment from imprisonment to branding on the right thumb. Montgomery admitted to his lawyer that it was he who started the Boston Massacre by shouting to the soldiers to fire and it was he who fired the first shot, with the other soldiers following.

John Adams later called his defense of the British soldiers "one of the most gallant, generous, manly, and disinterested actions of my whole life, and one of the best pieces of service I ever rendered my country." He cared more about justice than about a chance to rally the colonists against the British. John Adams demonstrated justice towards his enemies, despite the fact that his action made him unpopular among his fellow Boston patriots for some time.

Questions

1. Did John Adams actually witness the Boston Massacre?
2. Why were tensions so high in Boston?
3. Think of a situation where you have seen people react with emotion instead of being level-headed, and tell how some of the colonists and some of the British reacted wrongly.
4. What incident precipitated the Boston Massacre?
5. What was Captain Preston's dilemma?
6. How many people died in the Boston Massacre?
7. Who claimed to have started the Boston Massacre by hollering for men to fire?
8. Why did John Adams agree to represent Captain Preston?
9. How did Adams uphold justice?
10. Think of a situation that happened to you where you had to uphold justice even though it was difficult.

Virtue

DEFINITION

Maintaining moral excellence
and setting godly standards

MEMORY VERSE

That no man go beyond and defraud
his brother in any matter: because
that the Lord is the avenger of all such,
as we also have forewarned
you and testified.
For God hath not called us unto
uncleanness, but unto holiness.

I Thessalonians 4:6, 7

Weapons of War

Rev. Jacob Duché

Philadelphia, Pennsylvania
September 7, 1774

The British had rushed to land more troops in the Massachusetts Bay Colony. Armed with an order from Parliament, they moved to close Boston Harbor, bringing the city's bustling trade to an abrupt halt. As tensions simmered farther south in Virginia, fifty-six delegates from twelve of the thirteen colonies met in Philadelphia, Pennsylvania, to discuss the possibility of resolving issues between America and Great Britain before it was too late. The thirteenth, newest and smallest colony, Georgia, abstained, still hoping to receive help from Britain in quelling Native American attacks on the edge of the frontier. Last year, Benjamin Franklin had suggested calling together a meeting in response to the passing of the Coercive Acts (Intolerable Acts) by British Parliament, laws that the American colonists viewed as an effort on the part of the Crown to humiliate and subjugate the colonies. When the authorities closed the port, each colonial legislature rushed its delegates to Philadelphia for an emergency meeting.

White-wigged Quakers, sandy-haired southern delegates, and veteran leaders of northern Committees of Correspondence crowded into Carpenter's Hall in Philadelphia on September 6, 1774, to call for a Continental Congress the following day. When someone proposed opening the Congress with a prayer for guidance, John Jay of New York and Edward Rutledge of South Carolina jumped to their feet. We object to having prayer, they stated, since so many different religious affiliations will be present. There were Episcopalians, Presbyterians, Congregationalists, Quakers, and Anabaptists.

Then Samuel Adams, one of the foremost patriot leaders in Boston, rose to his full six-and-a-half foot height. Looking around at the other members present, he declared that since he was not a bigot, he would be glad to hear a prayer from any man of piety who was also a patriot. Although he had never visited Philadelphia before, Adams said that he had heard that the Reverend Jacob Duché was such a man. Perhaps, Adams suggested, they could get him

Reverend Jacob Duché

to read the prayers tomorrow. With these words, the Boston leader brought the dissenting delegates together and reminded them that the most important qualities at this time were not denomination or sect, but patriotism and faith. Someone seconded the motion and it passed in the affirmative.

September 7 dawned, an early autumn day. Delegates walked carefully through the Philadelphia streets before slipping into the meeting place. They had to meet in secret. If the British caught wind of the fact that known patriot leaders had gathered together to meet, the authorities would undoubtedly try them for treason. Hurrying from Christ Church just two blocks away on Second and Market Streets, thirty-seven-year-old Reverend Jacob Duché arrived at Carpenter Hall. Duché wore flowing Episcopalian vestments. His wide, white wig framed calm eyes and a thin face as serious as a judge's. At nine o'clock sharp, he mounted to the dais and opened the Episcopalian service book for the day. The roomful of delegates fell silent in anticipation. Jacob Duché looked down and began to read Psalm 35.

"Contend, O LORD, with those who contend with me; fight against those who fight against me. Take up shield and buckler; arise and come to my aid. Brandish spear and javelin against those who pursue me. Say to my soul, 'I am your salvation.'"

Duché's Huguenot ancestors had fled to William Penn's Quaker sanctuary in America to avoid persecution. Many of the men in this room had grandparents or great-grandparents who had sought religious liberty in a new land. Now the descendents of these pilgrims and pioneers wanted civil freedom as well. Now, the British had closed Boston Harbor, signaling a new, hostile attitude towards the colonies. Pressures with the British mounted on every side as colonists objected to the harsh tone of the Coercive Acts. Reverend Jacob Duché finished reading the Psalm, but he did not leave his place.

Suddenly, Duché closed his eyes and burst into extemporaneous prayer.

"O Lord our Heavenly Father, high and mighty King of kings, and Lord of lords, who dost from Thy throne behold all the dwellers on earth and reignest with power supreme and uncontrolled over all the Kingdoms, Empires and Governments; look down in mercy, we beseech Thee, upon these our American States, who have fled to Thee from the rod of the oppressor and thrown themselves on Thy gracious protection, desiring henceforth to be dependent only on Thee. To Thee have they appealed for the righteousness of their cause; to Thee do they now look up for that countenance and support, which Thou alone canst give. Take them, therefore, Heavenly Father, under Thy nurturing care; give them wisdom in Council and valour in the field; defeat the malicious designs of our cruel adversaries. Convince them of the unrighteousness of their Cause and if they persist in their sanguinary purposes, O! let the voice of Thy unerring justice sounding in their hearts constrain them to drop the weapons of war from their unnerved hands in the day of battle!"

His voice surged through the quiet hall of Congress, rising and falling in awe, now trembling with entreaty, now warm with thanksgiving.

"Be Thou present, O God of Wisdom, and direct the councils of this honorable assembly; enable them to settle things upon the best and surest foundation, that the scene of blood may be speedily closed; that order, harmony and peace may be effectually restored, and truth and justice, religion and piety, prevail and flourish amongst Thy people. Preserve the health of their bodies and vigor of their minds; shower down on them and the millions they represent, such temporal blessings as Thou seest expedient for them in this world, and crown them with everlasting glory in the world to come. All this we ask in the name and through the merits of Jesus Christ, Thy Son, our Savior, Amen."

Ten minutes came and went. Then Duché's voice died away. The men were struck speechless with his fervor and ardor. John Adams could not contain his emotion when he heard this prayer uttered with such "earnestness and pathos, and in a language so elegant and sublime." Duché knelt down in the hush and there was a sound of shuffling all around him as the entire room of delegates followed his example. George Washington was on his knees. In another corner, red-haired Patrick Henry bowed his head. Across the room, James Randolph, Richard Henry Lee, John Jay, and others knelt also.

Everyone began praying aloud for America, for Congress and Massachusetts, and particularly for besieged Boston. Tears ran down their faces. Drops glittered in the eyes of the Quakers present. As they rose from their knees, one delegate exclaimed that Duché was "worth riding a hundred miles to hear."

A short time later, Reverend Jacob Duché was appointed as the first chaplain of the United States Congress. Since that day, every session of Congress has opened with prayer. Jacob Duché demonstrated virtue by using the weapon of prayer to ask God's protection and guidance.

Take them, therefore, Heavenly Father, under Thy nurturing care; give them wisdom in Council and valour in the field; defeat the malicious designs of our cruel adversaries....

—Reverend Jacob Duché

Questions

1. What happened to cause the delegates to call for an emergency meeting?
2. Where did they meet?
3. What was the objection to opening the meeting in prayer?
4. By whom and how was it resolved?
5. Who was chosen to lead in prayer?
6. What passage of Scripture did he read?
7. What was the substance of his prayer?
8. How were the patriots affected by his prayer?
9. To what office did they appoint Rev. Duché?
10. What pattern did his example set for our Congress?
11. What godly standards might you be instrumental in setting a pattern for at church?

Dependability

DEFINITION

Honoring your word and responsibilities even if it means unexpected sacrifice

MEMORY VERSE

He sweareth to his own hurt,
and changeth not.

Psalm 15:4b

Midnight Ride

Wentworth Cheswell

Exeter & Portsmouth Harbor,
New Hampshire
December 15, 1774

He came out of the candlelit meeting into the cold winter night. Behind him, the meeting of the Provincial Committee of Safety at Exeter began to break up. Wentworth Cheswell, a thirty-year-old free Black man, made a rapid decision. Tonight, the members of the committee had received word that the British were on the move towards Portsmouth Harbor to attack the town. He knew that he had to get there and he had to leave now. Two other men, a Boston silversmith named Paul Revere and young William Dawes rode in a westerly direction.

Wentworth Cheswell rides to Portsmouth

A courier for the Committee of Safety, one of the local groups established throughout the colonies to supervise the public welfare, Cheswell regularly smuggled messages between Newmarket and Exeter. He might slip through to Portsmouth alive, or he might run into a detachment of Redcoats. His light brown face tense, Wentworth Cheswell moved into the night.

The British intended to attack Portsmouth Harbor by sea. Already someone had sighted the frigate Scarborough and the Canseau sloop of war in full sail. When the Committee of Safety in Newmarket received desperate messages begging the nearby colonies for aid against the British, they gathered an emergency meeting. Tonight, at the larger Exeter meeting, the committee decided to send thirty men from Newmarket to help the townspeople of Portsmouth Harbor. Carrying the vital information as to where the Newmarket militiamen would be sent in view of an impending attack, Cheswell made ready for an all-night ride.

Now, as he flung his leg over his horse's back and galloped north, Cheswell knew that no one else could warn the town. It was up to him. Trees and lonely houses rushed past. Sometimes a solitary yellow light blinked in the darkness. Most rural people had gone to bed early, snuffing out their tallow candles with pewter tongs or sleeping with windows shut tight against the cold. Cheswell slipped by the sleeping farmsteads, the sound of horse's hooves loud on the empty road. Every minute, he could expect to run into a regiment of British soldiers on the march. Usually, one could hear their rhythmic marching from some distance away. But there was always a chance that he would round a bend at full gallop, straight into the arms of a British grenadier. Straining his eyes and ears in the dark, Cheswell concentrated on the passing miles that brought him closer to his goal.

A highly educated man for his time, Wentworth Cheswell knew both Latin and Greek. At Dummer Academy, he excelled in swimming, horsemanship, reading, writing, and arithmetic. As a schoolmaster with five young children, he became a prosperous landowner in nearby Newmarket by age twenty-one. Now he owned thirty acres of land and his own pew in the church. Over the past few years, the town demonstrated such trust in Cheswell that they elected him town constable—the first Black man to hold public office in America. Two years later, they voted him in as selectman, making him a town father entrusted with the people's welfare and the head of local government in Newmarket.

He galloped on through the glassy, cold silence, not sparing his lathered horse or his tired body. His wife, Mary, must wonder what had become of him. She would have put Paul, Thomas, Samuel, and Mary to bed by now. But he had to finish this task.

The miles passed as dawn brightened the sky and he rode into the streets of Portsmouth Harbor. Sliding from his horse, Wentworth Cheswell gasped out his directions. He had ridden all night. Realizing that armed militiamen were on their way, the towns-people hurried to form defenses and blockade the British navy. As he stood there, exhausted and hungry in the light of day, Cheswell could have decided to turn around and head for home. Instead, he pulled himself together and hurried down to the wharf. There, he pitched in and helped build rafts in preparation for the British attack. Then they waited for the worst to happen. But the ocean remained calm. No warships appeared on the horizon. Later, Cheswell learned that the British attacked further to the west, the place where Paul Revere went. Due to this twist of events, Paul Revere received credit for the ride, while Wentworth Cheswell's heroic act went largely unknown.

Later, along with one hundred sixty-two other men, Cheswell signed the Association Test in April, 1776. In it, he pledged his life and property to take up arms against the British army and navy, which had begun hostile military movements. The men's signatures went before the committee drafting the Declaration of Independence. When men like John Hancock and Thomas Jefferson saw the number of signatures affixed to the Association Test, it gave them the courage to go forward and declare independence, knowing that the bulk of the country stood behind them. By his willingness to serve his country, Wentworth Cheswell demonstrated dependability by fulfilling his responsibilities despite the fact that it meant unexpected sacrifice.

The legacy of Wentworth Cheswell is a lasting one: a patriot, teacher, and church leader; an historian, archeologist, and educator; a judge and official elected to numerous offices (he is considered the first Black American elected to office in America). He is truly one of our forgotten patriots but he is a laudable example for all Americans.

—David Barton, Wallbuilders

Questions

1. How did Wentworth Cheswell demonstrate dependability even when it required extra sacrifice?
2. What news was he carrying?
3. What risk was he taking?
4. How did he show dependability beyond what was expected of him when he arrived at his destination?
5. What responsibilities do you have that others depend upon you to fulfill?
6. How could you determine to show increased dependability in your home?
7. Think of an example of someone who has been dependable and you have benefited from as a result.

Initiative

DEFINITION

Seeing a need and taking responsibility to meet it without being asked

MEMORY VERSE

Whatsoever thy hand
findeth to do,
do it with thy might.
Ecclesiastes 9:10a

Green Mountain Boys

Col. Ethan Allen

New York
May 10, 1775

A cold wind from Canada blew across Lake Champlain. On the eastern shore, thirty-eight-year-old Ethan Allen stared over the choppy water towards his target, the rotting old wooden British garrison. Fort Ticonderoga stood alone at the southern end of the lake. Darkness pressed in around the fort, wrapping the few guards and their women and children with sleep. He could not see any sentries. On fire at the recent news from Lexington and Concord after the first clash with the British, an irregular Connecticut militia had contacted Allen, asking for his help in capturing the British-held garrison at Fort Ticonderoga. The men of His Majesty's 26th Foot had no idea that the political situation had changed almost overnight, and that far from being the military authority in the American Colonies, they would soon come under attack.

From the windswept shoreline, Allen heard someone ride up on horseback—Captain Benedict Arnold. Arnold's icy voice rang out. He demanded to lead the expedition to glory. Swarming behind Arnold, the Green Mountain Boys, Allen's flushed

Colonel Ethan Allen discussing an upcoming battle

and angry woodsmen, threatened to mutiny if Allen gave into Arnold's demand. Bristling like a small turkey, Arnold launched into a violent tirade, but Allen, a big frontiersman with a cracked front tooth, refused to give in. The night was advancing, and Allen became annoyed with Arnold's insistent demands.

He swung round on his men. "What shall I do with the rascal?" he asked. "Put him under guard?"

"Better go side by side," someone suggested.

Arnold agreed with bad temper. A compromise meant that he would march with Allen at the head of the Green Mountain Boys, but he would not give any orders.

The dark waters of Lake Champlain lay before them, ruffled with squalls like the sea. Allen knew that they had to cross over to the western side to access the fort. Turning to his men, Allen sent out groups to commandeer boats from fishermen and farmsteads at the head of the lake. Hours passed, but no boats arrived. At last, Allen knew that he had to take the chance. Two boats lay offshore at Hand's Cove in Shoreham, and Allen stepped into one of them. Silently, his men piled into the boats. In the grey predawn, the lake and the tumbledown fort on the other side looked ghostly and alone.

Allen watched as the men dipped their oars into the chilly water, making little noise. He had spotted this strategic fort on his yearly trips to Canada to trade in Yankee horses and goods. Farmer, land-speculator and titular colonel of a rugged local mili-

Fort Ticonderoga

tia from the wilds of the New Hampshire land grants in what would become known as Vermont, Allen knew that it held eighty pieces of heavy artillery, twenty brass cannon and probably a dozen mortars, supported by small arms and other supplies. Only forty-five British soldiers held the fort. Five of them were old, worn-out or unserviceable men, a number of others sick.

The Green Mountain Boys knew how to fight. Over the past five years, these tough woodsmen formed local militia groups and drove surveyors and settlers off the land that they had disputed over, in court, with the royal Governor William Tryon and the powerful state of New York. Last year, the governor had placed a reward for one hundred pounds on Allen's head. After the news from Lexington and Concord, Benedict Arnold proposed that he capture the fort to the Committee of Public Safety. The Committee's Dr. Warren, fearful that an invading force involving any Green Mountain Boys from the New Hampshire grants would cause tension with the New York authorities, urged the committee to send Benedict Arnold and four hundred men on a "secret service" mission. Arnold started out, only to find that Allen's expedition, acting on his own initiative and backed by Connecticut money, had already left for Lake Champlain. With an uneasy truce established between the two men, Allen determined to go ahead with this "wolf hunt" against the British. The swift change in the political wind might bode well for Allen's dispute over the New Hampshire land grants, releasing their control from Governor Tryon and New York, and if so, the capture of a British fort would place him on the winning side.

Softly the two boats edged in to land. It was nearly 3 a.m. now. A faint paleness began to appear in the east. Allen did not hesitate. Only eighty-three of his men had landed and it would take much longer for the rest of them to find boats and paddle across. He could not afford to lose the element of surprise. Without waiting for the rest of his men, the big Hampshireman forged ahead down a road that wound through a thick northern forest. Skirting the edge of the lake, they came upon the east wall of the fort.

Allen, with Arnold jogging at his side, located an open wicket gate in the south wall. Both men raced through the gate just as a sleeping sentry awoke, lunged for his musket and fired. As it flashed in the pan, the sentry flung the gun away and bolted for

The capture of Fort Ticonderoga

cover through the entry to the fort. Another sentry charged at the colonists with his bayonet. But Allen hacked down with his sword and disarmed him.

"Where is the place where the commanding officer keeps?" he shouted.

The Green Mountain Boys poured through the gate. Halting on the parade ground, they lined up, shoulder to shoulder and back to back, yelling and whooping.

Meanwhile, Lieutenant Jocelyn Feltham, second in command at Fort Ticonderoga, sound asleep on the top floor of the barracks, sprang to his feet in horror as cries and screams of "No quarter, no quarter!" split the air. The fort was under attack. Rushing out without dressing, the lieutenant pounded on Captain William Delaplace's door. But he found the door locked. Unable to rouse the captain, he bolted back to the barracks and reached for a pair of trousers. Holding them up with one hand, he made a dash for the rear staircase leading past Captain Delaplace's room. As he struggled to break open the commander's door, Feltham saw frontiersmen climbing the bastions of the wing of the fort just outside. Desperately, Feltham tried to force his way through to his own men below. As he opened the back door leading downstairs, the foot of the stairs filled with Green Mountain Boys forcing their way up. Feltham tried to shout over the noise, but no one heard him. Finally, he waved his hand negatively, telling them not to come up. At this, Allen's men paused. The noise died down. Bravely, the officer began asking them random questions, hoping to give his soldiers time to fire back.

Ethan Allen pushed up the stairs, shouting: “Come out of there, all of you!”

Facing Lieutenant Feltham, Allen declared that he had orders from the province of Connecticut to seize Fort Ticonderoga. He intended to take possession of the fort and everything belonging to the crown of George III.

As he spoke, Allen held the sharp blade of his sword over the officer’s head. Crouching at the ready, his Boys kept their firelocks trained on his chest. When Feltham protested, they shouted that he was the commanding officer and should surrender the fort immediately. If a single British soldier fired, they warned, not a single man, woman or child in the fort would be left alive. At this, Arnold forced his way through the crowd to the stairs. His voice elegant and persuasive, he spoke for some time but without any success. Feltham insisted that as a loyal officer he could not surrender the fort on his own authority. When the Green Mountain Boys finally found out that he was not the commander of the fort, Feltham blocked them with his body from rushing upstairs to accost the captain.

Finally, Captain Delaplace, now dressed, came out to the head of the stairs. Allen would later claim that he rushed out, holding up his trousers with one hand. But while Feltham had only seconds to pull on a pair of breeches, the captain had time to get dressed during the uproar. Feltham, still holding up his breeches with one hand, was thrown into the captain's room under guard. The captain, pushed roughly downstairs, found to his humiliation, that all of his men had been caught asleep in bed. Allen ordered him to surrender at once. As the pale dawn seeped into the fort, the British commander stared at the self-styled American colonel.

"By what authority have you entered His Majesty's fort?" he asked.

Allen thundered: "In the name of the Great Jehovah and the Continental Congress!"

The captain surrendered the fort immediately. The cannons from Fort Ticonderoga were sent on ahead to aid General Washington's army which had begun the siege of Boston.

Ethan Allen demonstrated initiative by going ahead and pursuing a goal without waiting for others to do it for him or being hampered by a lack of resources.

Ever since I arrived to a state of manhood ... I have felt a sincere passion for liberty ... so that the first ... attempt at Lexington, to enslave America, thoroughly electrified my mind, and fully determined me to take part with my country.

—Ethan Allen

Questions

1. Why did Ethan Allen want to capture Fort Ticonderoga? How would it benefit the cause?
2. What was Arnold's motive in being involved?
3. What truce did Allen and Arnold reach?
4. How many men did Allen proceed with?
5. How did Allen's men capture the fort?
6. By whose authority did Allen proclaim to have entered the fort?
7. What was confiscated from the Fort and where was it sent to aid the colonists?
8. How did Ethan Allen demonstrate initiative?
9. What needs to be done in your home that you could demonstrate initiative by doing before being asked?

Faithfulness

DEFINITION

Acting upon an unshakable confidence in God

MEMORY VERSE

Watch ye, stand fast in the faith, quit you like men, be strong.

I Corinthians 16:13

Glory

Rev. Lemuel Haynes

Fort Ticonderoga, New York
May 19, 1775
South Granville, New York
September, 1833

They crept through the grey morning mist that shrouded the ghostly shores of Lake Champlain, blurring its outlines and sheltering their approach from the British sentinels stationed at the fort. In the early hours before dawn, the Green Mountain Boys entered the fort by a neglected gate, taking the guard by surprise. The patriot commander, Ethan Allen, bounded up the stairs to confront Captain William Delaplace and demanded his surrender. As the British officer stumbled out in his nightclothes, a group of militiamen stood below, waving the Green Mountain Boys' flag. Twenty-two-year-old Lemuel Haynes, an emancipated slave, watched too, his round, light brown face tense with excitement. He had seen a small piece of American soil seized from British hands and turned over to the cause of liberty.

He could not remember his mother. Sometimes her face, like a white blur, hovered over him, probing at his consciousness. He never knew his father, an African slave of mixed descent. At five months old, his well-to-do mother abandoned him, putting him out to service as an indentured servant at come of age to Deacon David Ross of Middle Granville, Massachusetts. He worked for Ross as an agricultural laborer for the next twenty-one years.

During those long years of drudgery, Haynes learned to read and devoured every book he could get his hands on. He read by the light of the fire, turning the pages of the Bible and thick tomes of theology. Sitting beside his master and listening to the harsh Calvinist sermons, the young man quickly developed his own views. One night, Haynes saw strange bluish-green, red, and purple lights float like stretching fingers across the sky. He had never heard of the northern phenomenon known as the Aurora Borealis. Terrified, he fell to his knees, believing that the Day of Judgment had arrived. Soon afterwards, Haynes became a Christian. Rejoicing in his new faith, he began preaching during services at the town parish.

Reverend Lemuel Haynes

His time of indentured service ended in 1774, just before tensions between Great Britain and the colonies erupted into full-scale war. Seeing the storm approaching, Haynes immediately enlisted in the local Granville militia. When the news of the bloody battles at Lexington and Concord in April, 1775, reached him, Haynes sat down and passionately scribbled out a long ballad-sermon describing the patriots' exploits. Copying out the title page in black ink, he called himself, "Lemuel a young [man]…, who obtained what little knowledge he possesses, by his own Application to letters." When the American colonies declared their independence, Lemuel Haynes temporarily gave up his plans to enter the ministry. Instead, he donned a militia uniform, picked up a musket, and marched to join his fellow town militiamen at Roxbury, Massachusetts.

Lemuel Haynes joined the ranks of the five thousand African American soldiers, both slave and free, who fought in the Continental Army during the Revolutionary War. In 1776, Haynes and his fellow militiamen set out to help garrison the captured Fort Ticonderoga. He served faithfully throughout the battles of Washington's northern campaign until after the Battle of Saratoga, when the arrival of French aid caused the theatre of war to shift to the south. Haynes admired George Washington and regularly preached sermons on the commander-in-chief's birthday. His war finished, Lemuel Haynes went home to Middle Granville, Massachusetts, where he married Elizabeth Babbitt, a young white schoolteacher. Following the war, in 1785, Haynes received his ordination as a Congregational minister. He became the first Black preacher to pastor a white congregation in the United States. He was also the first African American in the United States to receive an honorary Master's Degree, from Middlebury College, in 1804.

After forty-eight years of faithful ministry, pastoring two churches in Vermont and New York, Lemuel Haynes fell ill with a long and painful gangrenous disease. As he lay on his deathbed, the eighty-year-old Black minister glowed with joy and peace. "I have been examining myself and looking back on my past life, but I can find nothing in myself and nothing in all my past services to recommend me at the bar of Jehovah," he told a visitor. "Christ is my all. His blood is my only hope of acceptance. I have been praying for the faith of assurance, and feel that I have almost attained it ... I long to be in heaven. Oh! What blessed company will be there! I shall see there not only many great and good men whom I have seen and loved on the earth, but ... I shall see Abraham, and the prophets, and apostles, in the kingdom of glory! These men I have revered on the earth, and hope to see and converse with them in yonder brighter world."

The visitor asked him whether he had peace about letting go of the world. The old man's voice shook with emotion, "I know in whom I have believed, and I am not afraid to trust myself in His hands." He paused. "I have been preaching love to God and submission to His will for almost fifty years, and I have no idea of undoing what I have been trying to do almost my whole life." During this time, Haynes spoke to his sons and daughters on the subject of eternity. Finally, his son asked, "Father, is death a terror to you?"

A smile spread across the minister's face. "It has been rising of fifty years since I have been preparing for this, and do you think that I shall now shrink back? No—no!"

After this, the sun seemed to sink slowly down inside of him. At one point, as he lay silently in bed, he noticed one of his daughters, who did not believe in Christ, sitting nearby. He motioned for her to come closer. Catching her hand in his, he spoke to her in a weak whisper. Tears ran down her face. "Father, pray for me after you get to heaven," she choked.

Knowing that no person except Christ could pray for a sinner to the Father, Haynes exclaimed, "No, no!" Suddenly, he sighed, "What wonderful views I have had this day! I have been brought to the borders of the grave. Oh, what views! Wonderful! Wonderful! Wonderful! I have heard singing. Oh! How wonderful! I am well. Glory ineffable."

The next day, he seemed to enter a dark valley, different than the rugged countryside that he marched through as a militiaman during the Revolutionary War. Suddenly, he stretched out his hand. "Oh! What beauties I have seen!" he exclaimed. "Glories of the other world! What joys do I feel! I have seen the Savior." Then he whispered, "I love my wife, I love my children, but I love my Savior better than all." Finally, at three o'clock, on September 28, 1833, Lemuel Haynes fell asleep for the last time.

Lemuel Haynes demonstrated faithfulness both as an earthly soldier in the Continental Army and for nearly fifty years as a soldier of Christ. In his last letter to his children, he exhorted them to remain faithful: "I commit it all to God. Oh! Remember your Creator! Let not the fashions of the world divert your minds from eternity!"

The man who meanly will submit to wear a shackle, contemns the noblest gift of Heaven, and impiously affronts the God that made him free.

—Dr. Joseph Warren; An oration; delivered March sixth, 1775. At the request of the inhabitants of the town of Boston.

Questions

1. How did Lemuel Haynes become a Christian?
2. What plans did Lemuel postpone to join the militia?
3. What man did Lemuel admire? What did he do on this man's birthday each year?
4. What did Lemuel tell a visitor about his thoughts about dying?
5. How did Lemuel Haynes demonstrate faithfulness in both the Continental Army and to his Savior?
6. Can you think of a situation in your life in which you could practice faithfulness? to your family? church? Lord?

Steadfastness

DEFINITION

Unwavering or determined
in purpose

MEMORY VERSE

Therefore, my beloved brethren,
be ye stedfast, unmoveable, always
abounding in the work of the Lord,
forasmuch as ye know that your
labour is not in vain in the Lord.

I Corinthians 15:58

Sacrifice

Dr. Joseph Warren

Boston, Massachusetts
March 3, 1775 & June 17, 1775

They filled the Old South Church, standing in the pews, crowding the aisles, pushing against the pulpit stairs, and pressing into the pulpit itself. Thirty-four-year-old Dr. Joseph Warren, a member of the Massachusetts Committee of Correspondence, glanced towards the church entrance. He could hear the rumble of British accents; feel the deadly stirrings beneath the silence. They would kick him out if he tried to come in through the front door. Quickly, Warren made up his mind, scrambling into

Dr. Joseph Warren

the church through a pulpit window in the rear.

Straightening his shoulders, the young, boyish-faced doctor stepped into the pulpit. A hundred Redcoat officers and men stared coldly back at him. A heckler called out, his taunting voice bouncing off the walls. Warren raised his voice. Today marked the fifth anniversary of the Boston Massacre. He made his audience, filled with soldiers and colonists, see the snow spattering the March streets, the crowd gathering as the British troops grew ugly. Shots rang out. Crispus Attucks, a free Black dockworker tumbled to the ground. Then a second man fell bleeding onto the cobbles. Warren felt danger vibrating round him as he spoke. The air throbbed with tension as he loudly proclaimed the criminal acts perpetrated by the British.

Suddenly, a British officer sitting on the pulpit steps grimly held up several pistol bullets in his open palm. Warren knew what it meant. If he made the slightest slip, lost his nerve and provoked him to rage, the officer would shoot him where he stood. The act might lead to a massacre of other patriot leaders. Not a single muscle quivered in Warren's face. Glancing over at the officer, and still speaking steadily, he quietly walked up to the officer, and dropped a white handkerchief into the officer's hand. Confused by the courteous gesture, the officer accepted the handkerchief. He made no further move to disrupt Warren's speech that day.

Warren left the Old South Church that spring day, having proved his steadfastness to the patriot cause. Despite his busy medical practice in Boston, the doctor, a Harvard graduate, found the time to serve not only as one of the Sons of Liberty, but as president of the Provincial Congress—the highest post in the revolutionary government. Besides delivering brave orations commemorating

Dr. Warren speaking to General Putnam about joining the battle as a private soldier

the 1770 Boston Massacre, Warren drafted the "Suffolk Resolves." The Continental Congress approved his resolves, which urged resistance to Parliament's Coercive or Intolerable Acts. In 1774, Warren still hoped that the colonies might resolve their issues with Great Britain without resorting to war. By the next year, however, all such hope had vanished. Parliament rejected the "Olive Branch Petition," submitted by the colonies and sent additional British troops to American shores.

At home, Warren's fiancée, Mercy Scollay, looked after his four young motherless children, ranging from ages three to ten. They met when she came to him as a patient after his wife died three years before. Their relationship grew and blossomed, and by the spring of 1775, they considered themselves "unofficially engaged." He also wrote and published a song, titled "Free America," and set it to the popular English tune, "The British Grenadiers."

On the afternoon of April 18, 1775, Warren, as a member of the Committee of Correspondence, called for Paul Revere and William Dawes to ride and spread the alarm that the British garrison in Boston had mobilized for a raid on the nearby town of Concord. According to Warren's secret informant, probably Mrs. Margaret Gage, her husband, General Thomas Gage, not only determined to destroy the colonial munitions in Concord but to arrest patriot

The Battle of Bunker Hill

leaders, John Hancock and Sam Adams. Revere and Dawes set out over the moonlit road to Lexington to warn the two men to escape. Warren managed to slip out of Boston at dawn on April 19. When the battles of Lexington and Concord broke out later that same day, the doctor organized his militia and deployed them beside Brigadier General William Heath's men, forcing the Redcoats to retreat towards Boston. The British scrambled along the road from Concord with Warren hard on their heels. His men hung on the British rear, harassing and attacking their flanks like a pack of dogs. Bullets whipped past Warren's head. Suddenly, a musket ball clipped off a piece of his wig, just missing his skull. Panting, he drew up and watched as the British fled.

Soon after, his mother, hurrying up to Warren, saw his disfigured wig. She burst into tears and begged him not to risk his life.

"Where danger is, dear mother," Warren replied quietly, "there must your son be. Now is not the time for any of America's children to shrink from any hazard. I will set her free or die."

During the next few months, the doctor set to work to recruit and organize soldiers to take part in the Siege of Boston. On June 14, 1775, the Massachusetts Provincial Congress promoted him to a major general.

On June 17, the British under General Gage attacked the patriots' position on Breed's Hill, later known as Bunker Hill. Warren arrived in the middle of the smoke and heat. Militiamen, forming combat lines, jostled into position behind the barricades on the hill. Quickly and sharply, Warren demanded to know where the heaviest fighting was. General Israel Putnam pointed towards the redoubt on Breed's Hill. Seizing a musket, Warren turned to join the men as a private soldier. General Putnam, General Artemus Ward, and Colonel William Prescott tried to stop him. They protested that he had no military education or experience. They begged him to serve instead as a commander. Warren shook his head. Both Putnam and Prescott had combat experience, so he felt unqualified to take command. He could only inspire the men to hold their ground against overwhelming numbers. Shouldering his musket, Warren scrambled up to join the men crouching in the hot sun behind the barricades.

Like a cloud passing over the sky, casting huge, chilly shadows on the landscape, Warren knew that he would die. The premonition touched him earlier that day when he saw Betsy Palmer, whose husband had fought at Lexington. All at once, he turned to her and exclaimed: "… I shall go to the hill and I shall never come off."

Meanwhile, miles away in Worchester, Mercy sheltered his small children from the Siege of Boston. He had no time to think of them, no time for regrets. He felt only the smoke stinging his eyes, heard the yells, and felt the musket blistering his hands. Now the whole British army came at them, roaring, swarming up the slope. The patriots beat them back with difficulty. After regrouping below, the British troops moved into line for another attack. Warren encouraged the men to stand firm. He kept repeating: "These fellows say we won't fight! By Heaven, I hope I shall die up to my knees in blood!"

They came on again, in a third wave. British marines stormed the rebel position as the defilade guns grew silent. A single patriot gun echoed here and there as the militiamen began to retreat. Out of ammunition, Warren remained in the redoubt, facing the assault in order to give his men time to escape. As the Redcoats cleared the rise, he did not see the musket leveled at the back of his head, or Lieutenant Lord Rawdon's grim face behind it. In a single instant, the musket ball blacked out his vision. Mercy's face, his children's prattle, the hot sun glittering on the redoubt disappeared. The shouts of his men grew dimmer. Then the world stopped for him.

Afterwards, British soldiers combing the field stripped his body and bayoneted it beyond recognition. Finally, they tumbled his body into a shallow ditch. British Captain Walter Laurie later boasted that he "stuffed the scoundrel with another rebel into one hole, and there he and his seditious principles may remain." The shooting on Breed's Hill had lasted less than an hour before the patriots ran out of ammunition. Although technically a British victory, Gage had lost so many men during the three assaults that it proved a hollow victory.

Ten months after Warren's death, his brother John, who served as a surgeon at Bunker Hill, and Paul Revere exhumed his body. Paul Revere recognized his friend by a tooth he had made for him, an act that might be the "first recorded instance of post-mortem identification by forensic odontology in early Colonial America." Before they moved Warren's body to the Granary Burying Ground, his grieving fiancée, Mercy Scollay, had brought his four children into her own home. She cared for "these dear little ones," as she called them, gathering support for their education from the Sons of Liberty and even the Continental Congress, until she lost custody of them to Warren's family.

General Gage afterwards remarked that Warren's death proved equal to the death of five hundred men. Today, fourteen states have a Warren County named in his honor, and five ships in the Continental and United States Navy have also carried his name.

Before his death, Joseph Warren wrote: "It is an indispensable duty which we owe to God, our country, ourselves, and posterity, by all lawful ways and means in our power, to maintain, defend, and preserve those civil and religious rights and liberties for which many of our fathers fought, bled, and died, and to hand them down entire to future generations." Warren demonstrated steadfastness to the Revolution, causing the American colonists to view him as a martyr. Seventy years later, the Bunker Hill Monument Association erected a monument on Bunker Hill to the "memory of the brave men who fell there in the cause of human liberty."

Questions

1. What vocation did Joseph Warren practice?
2. What did he speak of in the Old South Church?
3. How did he calm the British officer?
4. What action on the part of the British government persuaded Dr. Warren to give up on resolving issues with Great Britain without resorting to war?
5. Who took care of Dr. Warren's children?
6. What role did Dr. Warren play in spreading the alarm on April 18, 1775?
7. What was Dr. Warren's response to his mother when she was upset at his close call with a musket ball?
8. Tell of Dr. Warren's experiences at the Battle of Bunker Hill.
9. What did Joseph Warren write concerning our duty to posterity?
10. How did Dr. Warren's involvement in the War for Independence demonstrate steadfastness?

Determination

DEFINITION

Purposing to exert all your energies in accomplishing a task regardless of the opposition

MEMORY VERSE

I have fought a good fight, I have finished my course, I have kept the faith: Henceforth there is laid up for me a crown of righteousness, which the Lord, the righteous judge, shall give me at that day: and not to me only, but unto all them also that love his appearing.

II Timothy 4:7-8

Providential Shot

Peter Salem

Boston, Massachusetts
June 17, 1775

The attack came at dawn. The colonists could see the British Marines forming at the base of Breed's (Bunker) Hill. Crouching behind the low defenses, Peter Salem, a twenty-five-year-old ex-slave, waited tensely. A few years before, he would not have been able to fight for his country under Massachusetts law. But now, as the need for soldiers increased due to tensions with Great Britain and the lawless frontier, the rules relaxed, allowing free African Americans to fight. Peter Salem's owner, Major Lawson Buckminster, gave Salem his freedom in exchange for his promise to fight with the colonial militia. Recruited by the Massachusetts Committee of Safety, the young man enlisted as a minuteman in Captain Drury's Company of Colonel Nixon's 6th Massachusetts Regiment. He saw his first action against the Redcoats at Concord in April.

Gravestone of Peter Salem, a Soldier of the Revolution

Musket fire rolled across the slopes, smashing into the Americans' thin ranks. General William Howe had ordered his British troops to pour three devastating volleys on the patriots. The heavy fire began pushing the Minutemen back across Bunker Hill. Suddenly, Salem noticed a lull in the firing, like the deadly calm before a savage storm. Below them, Major John Pitcairn positioned himself at the head of his British Marines for an attack.

All at once, they burst from the pale summer dawn. Salem, sighting over the defenses, fired steadily, even as the ammunition rapidly dwindled. The Marines came on, doggedly. Desperately, the Americans forced back two attacks, one after another. Then the British Marines threw themselves in a third and final assault against the patriot position on Breed's Hill.

The Americans had run out of bullets. As the Marines neared the crest of the hill, they began stuffing anything they could find into their muskets and pouring in powder. Leveling their guns over the breastworks, the Minutemen waited as the Redcoats came closer. Suddenly, a hail of broken glass, nails and metal shards ripped into the Marines' ranks, causing a drastic fifty percent casualty rate and more than one thousand British dead and wounded.

Pitcairn advanced on foot, personally leading the last attack. As they pressed towards the top of Breed's Hill, they ran into a second line of infantry that had just fallen back under the homemade patriot fire. Pitcairn kept shouting: "Break, and let the Marines through!"

Their muskets empty, some of the Americans began to fall back towards the north. As Redcoats scrambled over the low breastworks, Peter Salem spun around to fight. Men pitched forward on either side of him as the American casualties rose sharply to four hundred dead and wounded. Salem knew that they would not be able to fight their way out.

Suddenly, his worn, determined face appeared over the low breastworks. He sighted along the barrel of his gun. The Royal British Marines

"The Death of General Warren at the Battle of Bunker Hill" by John Trumbull
(Peter Salem may be pictured behind the officer with sword, bottom right.)

charged the barricade in a blur of red coats and acrid musket smoke. Major Pitcairn scrambled up the last rise, his two officer sons on either side. He came so close that Salem could see him waving his sword to his men. Pitcairn bellowed: "Now, for the glory of the Marines!" The patriots began to fall back from the fence under the Marines' sudden onslaught. Turning to his men, Pitcairn shouted: "The day is ours!" He demanded that the patriots surrender. Just then, Peter Salem squeezed the trigger and fired.

The musket ball struck Pitcairn in the chest. As he collapsed, his son, Lieutenant William Pitcairn, lifted him in his arms and dragged him out of the line of fire. Seeing their leader fall, the Marines faltered for a few stunned moments. While they milled in confusion, the battered Americans were able to retreat and escape. Major Pitcairn died a few hours later. It's believed that Peter Salem is in fact the Black man depicted on the right-hand side of John Trumbull's eighteenthth century drawing: "The Death of General Warren at the Battle of Bunker Hill." While the British ultimately won the conflict that became known as the Battle of Bunker Hill, Peter Salem's providential act of determination gave the Americans time to retreat and regroup, preventing a total annihilation of the budding American Revolution.

For the Lord GOD will help me; therefore shall I not be confounded: therefore have I set my face like a flint, and I know that I shall not be ashamed.

—Isaiah 50:7

Questions

1. How did Peter Salem obtain his freedom?
2. Tell about the Battle of Bunker Hill.
3. What happened to cause the Patriot side to lose the battle?
4. How did the Patriots show determination even when they ran out of ammunition?
5. What was Peter Salem's last act of determination?
6. Name someone you've read about in the Bible who has shown great determination.
7. What are some ways you could practice determination in your life?

Selected Bibliography

Adams, John, and L. H. Butterfield. *Diary and Autobiography of John Adams, Vol. II.* Cambridge: Harvard University Press, 1962.

Adams, Samuel. *The Life and Public Services of Samuel Adams,* William V. Wells, editor. Boston: Little, Brown, and Company, 1865, Vol. I, p. 504.

Aldridge, Alfred O. *Benjamin Franklin and Nature's God.* Durham, NC: Duke University Press, 1967.

Allison, Robert. *The Boston Massacre.* Beverly, MA: Applewood Books, 2006.

Amler, Jane Frances. *Haym Solomon: Patriot Banker of the American Revolution.* Powerkids Press, 2004.

Ammon, Richard. *Valley Forge.* Holiday House, 2006.

Anderson, Fred. *Crucible of War: The Seven Years' War and the Fate of Empire in British North America: 1754-1766.* New York: Alfred A. Knopf, 2000.

Archer, Richard. *As if an Enemy's Country: the British Occupation of Boston and the Origins of Revolution.* Oxford, NY: Oxford University Press, 2010.

Barton, Charles D. *The Bulletproof George Washington.* Wallbuilders Press, 1990.

Barton, David. *The Jefferson Lies.* Thomas Nelson, 2012

Beliles, Mark A. and Stephen K. McDowell. *America's Providential History.* Charlottesville, VA: Providence Foundation, 1989.

Bessette, Joseph M. and John J. Pitney, Jr. *American Government and Politics: Deliberation, Democracy and Citizenship*. Boston: Wadsworth Cengage Learning, 2011.

Billias, George Athan. *General John Glover and his Marblehead Mariners.* New York: Holt, Rinehart & Winston, 1960.

Bobrick, Benson. *Angel in the Whirlwind: The Triumph of the American Revolution.* New York: Simon & Schuster, 2011.

Bodie, Idella. *The Man Who Loved the Flag.* Heroes and Heroines of the American Revolution, 2008.

Bowdoin, James, Samuel Adams, et al. *A Short Narrative of the Horrid Massacre.* London: W. Bingley, 1770.

Bowen, Catherine Drinker. *Miracle at Philadelphia: The Story of the Constitutional Convention: May to September 1787.* New York: Book-of-the-Month Club, Inc., 1986.

Boyd, Julian P. and Gerard W. Gawalt. *The Declaration of Independence: The Evolution of the Text.* University Press of New England, 1999.

Brady, Patricia. *Martha Washington: An American Life.* New York: Viking Press, 2005.

Brandt, Clare. *The Man in the Mirror: A Life of Benedict Arnold.* New York: Random House, 1994.

Brookhiser, Richard. *James Madison.* Basic Books, 2011.

Brooks, Victor. *The Boston Campaign.* Conshohocken, PA: Combined Publishing, 1999.

Buchanan, John. *The Road to Valley Forge: How Washington Built the Army that Won the Revolution.* Wiley, 2004.

Burnett, Edward Cody. *The Continental Congress.* New York: Norton, 1941.

Burnham, Norman Hammond. *The Battle of Groton Heights: A Story of the Storming of Fort Griswold and the Burning of New London, on the Sixth of September, 1781.* Kessinger Publishing, 2006.

Carbone, Gerald M. *Nathanael Greene: A Biography of the American Revolution.* New York: Palgrave Macmillan, 2010.

Carstens, Kenneth C. and Nancy Son Carstens, eds. *The Life of George Rogers Clark, 1752-1818: Triumphs and Tragedies.* Westport, CT: Praeger, 2004.

Cheney, Lynne. *When Washington Crossed the Delaware: A Wintertime Story for Young Patriots.* New York: Simon & Schuster, 2012.

Chernow, Ron. *Washington: A Life.* New York: Penguin Press, 2010.

Clary, David A. *George Washington's First War: His Early Military Adventures.* New York: Simon & Schuster, 2011.

Coffin, Charles L. *The Boys of '76.* Weiner Media, 2009.

Collier, Christopher. *Decision in Philadelphia: The Constitutional Convention of 1787.* New York: Ballantine Books, 2007.

Collins, Kathleen. *Marquis de Lafayette: French Hero of the American Revolution.* Rosen Central, 2004.

Connecticut Society of the Sons of the American Revolution. *King George's Head.* Sons of the American Revolution, Winter, 1998.

Cooley, Timothy Mather. *Sketches of the Life and Character of the Reverend Samuel Haynes, A.M., for Many Years Pastor of a Church in Rutland, Vermont, and Late in Granville, New York.* New York: Negro Universities Press, 1969.

Copp, John J. *The Battle of Groton Heights: The Massacre of Fort Griswold; and the Burning of New London.* Groton Heights Centennial Committee, 1879.

Crocker, Thomas E. *Braddock's March: How the Man Sent to Seize a Continent Changed American History.* Westholme Publishing, 2011.

Crofut, W. A. and John M. Morris. *The Military and Civil History of Connecticut during the War of 1861-65.* Ledyard Bill, 1868.

Dameron, J. David. *Kings Mountain: The Defeat of the Loyalists, October 7, 1780.* Cambridge, MA: DaCapo Press, 2003.

Davis, Burke. *Black Heroes of the American Revolution.* Sandpiper, 1992.

Dawson, Thomas Fulton. *Life and Character of Edward Oliver Wolcott, Late a Senator of the United States From the State of Colorado.* Forgotten Books, 2012.

Derleth, August. *Vincennes: Portal to the West.* Englewood Cliffs, NJ: Prentice-Hall, 1968.

Dorson, Richard M., *Patriots of the American Revolution: True Accounts by Great Americans from Ethan Allen to George Rogers Clark.* New York: Gramercy Books, 1953.

Driver, Carl S. *John Sevier: Pioneer of the Old Southwest.* Chapel Hill: University of North Carolina Press, 1932.

Dunkerly, Robert M. *The Battle of King's Mountain: Eyewitness Accounts.* The History Press, 2007.

Field, Joseph E. *"Worthy Partner": The Papers of Martha Washington*. Praeger Press, 1994.

Finger, John R. *Tennessee Frontiers: Three Regions in Transition.* Indiana University Press, 2001.

Fischer, David Hackett. *Paul Revere's Ride.* New York: Oxford University Press, 1994. —. *Washington's Crossing.* Oxford University Press, 2006.

Fleming, Thomas. *Washington's Secret War: The Hidden History of Valley Forge.* Harper Perennial: 2006.

Flexner, James Thomas. *The Traitor and the Spy: Benedict Arnold and John Andre.* New York: Little, Brown & Company, 1975.

Foreman, Samuel A. *Dr. Joseph Warren: The Boston Tea Party, Bunker Hill, and the Birth of American Liberty.* New York: Pelican Publishing, 2011.

Freedman, Russell. *Washington at Valley Forge.* Holiday House: 2008.

Frothingham, Richard. *The Life and Times of Joseph Warren.* Applewood Books, 2009.

Fritz, Jean. *Why Not Lafayette?* New York: Puffin, 2001.

Garrison, Webb. *White House Ladies: Fascinating Tales and Colorful Curiosities.* Tennessee: Thomas Nelson Press, 1996.

Gingrich, Newt. *Valley Forge.* St. Martin's Griffin, 2011.

Golway, Terry. *Washington's General: Nathanael Greene and the Triumph of the American Revolution.* New York: Holt, 2005.

Goodrich, Charles A. *Lives of the Signers to the Declaration of Independence.* New York: Thomas Mather, 1832.

Gordon, William. *The History of the Rise, Progress, and Establishment, of the Independence of the United States of America.* Berkeley: University of California Collection, 1788.

Greene, George W. *The Life of Nathanael Greene, Major-General in the Army of the Revolution.* 3 vols. Freeport, NY: Books for Libraries Press, 1972.

Hall, Verna M. *The Christian History of the Constitution of the United States of America.* San Francisco: Foundation for American Christian Education, 1983.

Hanna, Willard A. *The Berkshire–Litchfield Legacy.* C. E. Tuttle and Company, 1984.

Harrison, Lowell H. *George Rogers Clark and the War in the West.* Lexington, KY: University of Kentucky Press, 2001.

Hatch, Robert McConnell. *Major John Andre: A Gallant in Spy's Clothing.* New York: Houghton Mifflin, 1986.

Haugen, Brenda. *Martha Washington: First Lady of the United States.* Compass Point Books: 2005.

Haw, James. " 'Every Thing Here Depends upon Opinion': Nathanael Greene and Public Support in the Southern Campaigns of the American Revolution." *South Carolina Historical Magazine,* 109 (July 2008): 212-31.

Heinemann, Ronald L., John G. Kolp, Anthony S. Parent, Jr., and William G. Shade. *Old Dominion, New Commonwealth: A History of Virginia, 1607-2007.* University of Virginia Press, 2007.

Hibbert, Christopher. *Redcoats and Rebels: The War for America 1770-1781.* Grafton Books, 1990

Hobson, Charles F. and Robert A. Rutlands, eds. *The Papers of James Madison: Volume 12, 2 March 1789-20 January 1790.* Charlottesville: University Press of Virginia, 1979.

Hogeland, William. *Declaration: The Nine Tumultuous Weeks When America Became Independent, May 1–July 4, 1776.* New York: Simon & Schuster, 2010.

Hopkins, Stephen. *The Grievances of the American Colonies Candidly Examined,* New York: Research Reprints Inc., 1970, first published London: J. Almon, 1766, pp. 45-48.

Hutchinson, Francis. *A Fair Account of the Late Unhappy Disturbance at Boston.* London: B. White, 1770.

Isaacson, Walter. *Benjamin Franklin: An American Life.* New York: Simon & Schuster, 2004.

Jefferson, Thomas. *Jefferson's "Bible"; The Life and Morals of Jesus of Nazareth XV-XVI.* ed. Judd Patton (Grove City): American Book Distributors, 1996.

Jefferson, Thomas. *The Writings of Thomas Jefferson, Vol. 9.* ed. Paul Leicester Ford. New York: G.P. Putnam's Sons, 1899.

Johnson, Clifton (1915). *The Picturesque Hudson.* MacMillan. Retrieved 2009-07-08.

Jones, Charles Colcock. *Sergeant William Jasper.* Kessinger Publishing, 2010.

Kaplan, Sidney, and Emma Nogrady Kaplan. *The Black Presence in the Era of the American Revolution.* Amherst, MA: The University of Massachusetts Press, 1989.

Ketcham, Ralph Louis. *James Madison: A Biography.* Charlottesville, VA: University of Virginia Press, 1971.

Ketchum, Richard M. *Saratoga: Turning Point of America's Revolutionary War.* New York: Henry Holt, 1997.

Kopperman, Paul. *Braddock at the Monongahela.* Pittsburgh, PA: University of Pittsburgh Press, 1977.

Krensky, Stephen. *DK Biography: Benjamin Franklin.* DK Children: 2007.

Labunski, Richard. *James Madison and the Struggle for the Bill of Rights.* New York Oxford: University Press, 2006.

Lane, Jason. *General and Madame de Lafayette: Partners in Liberty's Cause in the American and French Revolutions.* Taylor Trade Publishing, 2003.

Lindenmeyer, Otto. *Black & Brave: The Black Soldier in America.* New York, 1970.

Loane, Nancy K. *Following the Drum: Women at the Valley Forge Encampment.* Potomac Books, Inc., 2009.

Lockhart, Paul Douglas. *The Drillmaster of Valley Forge: the Baron de Von Steuben and the Making of the American Army.* New York: Harper Collins, 2008.

Lodge, Henry Cabot and Theodore Roosevelt. *Hero Tales from American History,* George Grant, ed. White Hall, WV: Tolle Lege Press, 2012.

Luzader, John F. *Saratoga: A Military History of the Decisive Campaign of the American Revolution.* New York: Savas Beatie, 2010.

Maier, Pauline. *American Scripture: Making the Declaration of Independence.* New York: Knopf, 1997.

Marshall, Peter and David Manuel. *The Light and the Glory.* Revell, 1977.

Martin, James Kirby. *Benedict Arnold, Revolutionary War Hero: An American Warrior Reconsidered.* New York: New York University Press, 1997.

Massachusetts Historical Society. *Henry Knox Diary, 20 November 1775 to 13 January 1776.*

Massey, Gregory D. *General Nathanael Greene and the American Revolution in the South.* University of South Carolina Press, 2012.

McClung, Robert. *Young George Washington and the French and Indian War, 1753-1758.* Linnet Books, 2002.

McCrady, Edward. *The History of South Carolina in the Revolution, 1775-1780.* New York: Macmillan, 1901.

McCullough, David. *1776.* New York: Simon & Schuster, 2005.

Messick, Hank. *King's Mountain: The Epic of the Blue Ridge "Mountain Men" in the American Revolution.* New York: Little & Brown, 1976.

Middlekauff, Robert. *The Glorious Cause: The American Revolution, 1763-1789.* New York and Oxford: Oxford University Press, 2007.

Milgrim, Shirley Gorson. *Haym Salomon: Liberty's Son.* The Jewish Publication Society, 1979.

Mintz, Max M. *The Generals of Saratoga: John Burgoyne and Horatio Gates.* New Haven, CT: Yale University Press, 1990.

Morrissey, Brendan. *Saratoga 1777: Turning Point of a Revolution.* Oxford: Osprey Publishing, 2000.

Morrill, Dan. *Southern Campaigns of the American Revolution.* Nautical & Aviation Publishing, 1993.

National Archives Education Staff. *The Constitution: Evolution of a Government.* Santa Barbara: ABC-CLIO, Inc., 2001.

Pancake, John. *This Destructive War.* University of Alabama Press, 1985.

Payan, Gregory. *Marquis de Lafayette: French Hero of the American Revolution.* The Rosen Publishing Group, 2002.

Peacock, Louise. *Crossing the Delaware: A History in Many Voices.* Aladdin, 2007.

Peters, Madison C. *Haym Salomon: The Financier of the Revolution.* University Press of the Pacific, 2005.

Puls, Mark. *Henry Knox: Visionary General of the American Revolution.* New York: Palgrave, 2010.

Randall, Henry Stephens. *The Life of Thomas Jefferson,* Vol. 3. New York: Derby & Jackson, 1858.

Randall, William Sterne. *Benedict Arnold: Patriot and Traitor.* Dorset Press, 2001.

Randall, Williard Sterne. *Ethan Allen: His Life and Times.* New York: W. W. Norton, 2011.

Reit, Seymour. *Guns for General Washington: A Story of the American Revolution.* Sandpiper, 2001.

Rosen, Gary. *American Compact: James Madison and the Problem of Founding.* Lawrence, KS: University Press of Kansas, 1999.

Russell, Charles Edward. *Haym Solomon and the Revolution.* Ayer Company Publishers, 1930.

Rutland, Robert Allen. *James Madison: The Founding Father.* Columbia, MO: University of Missouri Press, 1987.

Saillant, John. *Black Puritan, Black Republican: The Life and Thought of Lemuel Haynes, 1753-1833.* New York, Oxford University Press, 2003.

Savas, Theodore P., and Dameron, J. David. *A Guide to the Battles of the American Revolution.* Savas Beatie, 2005.

Scheer, George F. and Hugh F. Rankin, *Rebels and Redcoats.* New York: The World Publishing Company, 1957.

Schwartz, Laurens R. *Jews and the American Revolution: Haym Solomon and Others,* Jefferson, NC: McFarland & Co., 1987.

Scollay, Mercy to Elijah Dix. "I Wear a Face Foreign to the Feelings of My Heart" (Boston: April 26, 1776). *Mercy Scollay Papers, 1775-1824.* Cambridge Historical Society, Cambridge, Massachusetts.

Silverman, Jerry. *Of Thee I Sing.* Citadel Press, 2002.

Silvey, Anita. *Henry Knox: Bookseller, Soldier, Patriot.* Clarion Books, 2010.

Simpson, Andrew. "In St. Patrick's Shadow: The Peculiar Holiday of Evacuation Day," *The Bostonian Society News* (2004, Issue 1).

Steele, William O. *John Sevier: Pioneer Boy. The Childhood of Famous Americans Series.* Indianapolis: Bobbs-Merrill, 1953.

Stewart, David O. *The Summer of 1787: The Men Who Invented the Constitution.* New York: Simon & Schuster, 2008.

Sumner Letter, "Boston 1775," accessed on 02/08/2013.

Tonsetic, Robert. *1781: The Decisive Year of the Revolutionary War.* Casemate, 2011.

Uhlar, Janet. *Liberty's Martyr: The Story of Dr. Joseph Warren.* Dog Ear Publishing, 2009.

Unger, Harlow Giles. *Lafayette.* Hoboken, NJ: John Wiley & Sons, 2002.

Vile, John R. *The Constitutional Convention of 1787: A Comprehensive Encyclopedia of America's Founding.* 2 Vols. ABC-CLIO: 2005.

Walett, Francis. "James Bowdoin, Patriot Propagandist." *The New England Quarterly:* 23:3 (September 1950).

Ware, Susan. *Forgotten Heroes: Inspiring American Portraits from Our Leading Historians.* Portland, OR: Simon & Schuster, 2000.

Warren, Joseph. *The Suffolk Resolves,* September 9, 1774.

Washington, George to Martha Washington, "My Dearest Life and Love," June 24, 1776.

Washington, George to William Gordon. "8 July 1788." *Writings,* 27: 49-52.

Wheeler, Richard "Little Bear." *God's Mighty Hand: Providential Occurrences in World History.* Bulverde, TX: Mantle Ministries Press.

Wheeler, William Bruce, Susan Becker, and Lorri Glover. *Discovering the American Past: A Look at the Evidence: To 1877.* Belmont, CA: Cengage Learning, 2011.

White, Alain C. *The History of the Town of Litchfield, Connecticut, 1720-1920.* Litchfield, CT: Enquirer Print, 1920.

White, Richard. *Jordan Freeman Was My Friend.* Xlibris Corps, 2003 (Historical Fiction).

Wilson, Barry K. *Benedict Arnold: A Traitor in Our Midst.* McGill Queens Press, 2001.

York, Neil Longley. *The Boston Massacre: A History with Documents.* New York: Taylor & Francis, 2010.

Websites and Other Media

Brennan, Daniel. "Did James Madison suffer a nervous collapse due to the intensity of his studies?" Mudd Manuscript Library Blog, January 2008, Princeton University Archives and Public Policy Papers Collection, Princeton University.

Fowler, William M. "Glover, John." *American National Biography Online,* www.anb.org/ February 2000.

Garden, Alexander. *"Sergeant Jasper, 2nd Regiment." Anecdotes of the Revolutionary War in America. 1822.* http://books.google.com/books?id=WJ98ynQ-W-AC&pg=PA90

"Henry Knox and the 'Noble Train of Artillery'" on the *Fort Ticonderoga National Historic Landmark.* http://www.fort-ticonderoga.org/history/bibliographies/henry_knox.htm

"Heralds of a Liberal Faith," Volumes I-IV. http://harvardsquarelibrary.org/Heralds/Jonathan-Mayhew.php

Sevier, William Jay, and Lance Sevier. "The Life of John Sevier Time Line, Including Family Origins & World Events, 1506 -1815." http://www.johnsevier.com/jstime.html

"Saratoga National Historical Park." National Park Service. http://www.nps.gov/sara/.

Von Steuben's Continentals: The First American Army (Documentary DVD, Actor: John D. Pagano, Lionheart Filmworks, 2007).

Image Credits

Dependability

http://www.flickriver.com/photos/itinerant_wanderer/4023082606/

Determination

Death of General Warren: Public Domain. http://upload.wikimedia.org/wikipedia/commons/9/91/The_death_of_general_warren_at_the_battle_of_bunker_hill.jpg

Enthusiasm

Public Domain. Library of Congress. http://www.awesom-estories.com/images/user/5a3e5a8fd1.jpg

Faithfulness

Portrait of Rev. Lemuel Haynes: Public Domain. http://digitalgallery.nypl.org/nypldigital/dgkeysearchdetail.cfm?trg=1&strucID=580965&imageID=1232090&word=African%20American%20Baptists&s=3¬word=&d=&c=147&f=2&k=3&lWord=&lField=&sScope=Collection%20Guide&sLevel=&sLabel=Africana%20%26amp%3B%20Black%20History&sort=&total=179&num=20&imgs=20&pNum=&pos=39

Humility

Braddock's Retreat: Public Domain. http://en.wikipedia.org/wiki/File:FrenchAndIndianWar.jpg

Washington 1772: Public Domain. http://en.wikipedia.org/wiki/File:Washington_1772.jpg

French & Indian War battle: Public Domain. "Twenty Brave Men" by Jackson Walker. http://www.nationalguard.mil/resources/photo_gallery/heritage/hires/Twenty_Brave_Men.jpg

Initiative

Fort Ticonderoga: Public Domain. http://www.suite101.com/view_image_articles.cfm/551490

Ethan Allen, 1738-1789, full-length portrait, standing, before "the Green Mountain Boays in Council", examining map: Library of Congress Control Number 2005688179

Fort Ticonderoga: http://en.wikipedia.org/wiki/File:Ticonderoga1.jpg

Justice

John Adams Portrait: Public Domain. National Park Service: http://www.nps.gov/adam/images/20071211161151.jpg

Boston Massacre: Public Domain. National Archives, http://en.wikipedia.org/wiki/File:Boston_Massacre,_03-05-1770_-_NARA_-_518262.tif

Boston Massacre Aftermath: Public Domain. http://www.earlyamerica.com/earlyamericanimages/events1.html

Thomas Hutchinson: Public Domain. http://en.wikipedia.org/wiki/File:ThomasHutchinsonByEdwardTruman.jpg

Sons of Liberty symbol: Public Domain. http://revolutionarywartest.weebly.com/uploads/1/4/1/3/14137852/876961420.jpg

Samuel Adams: illustration by Linda J. Linder, *For You They Signed,* Marilyn Boyer, Rustburg, VA, The Learning Parent, 2008

Thomas Paine: Public Domain. http://en.wikipedia.org/wiki/File:Thomas_Paine_by_Laurent_Dabos-crop.jpg

Passion

Samuel Adams Portrait: Public Domain. http://en.wikipedia.org/wiki/File:J_S_Copley_-_Samuel_Adams.jpg

Boston Massacre: Public Domain. http://www.archives.gov/research/military/american-revolution/pictures/index.html#ne. Engraving by Paul Revere.

Hancock-Clarke House: http://en.wikipedia.org/wiki/File:Hancock-Clarke_House_Lexington_Massachusetts.jpg, Daderot, July, 2005

Steadfastness

Dr. Joseph Warren Portrait: Public Domain. http://en.wikipedia.org/wiki/File:JosephWarrenByCopley.jpeg

Warren offering to serve under Israel Putnam: Public Domain. http://en.wikipedia.org/wiki/File:WarrenPutnam.jpg

Battle of Bunker Hill: http://www.nationalguard.mil/resources/photo_gallery/heritage/hires/Whites_of_Eyes.jpg painting by Ken Riley, Copyright: The John F. Kennedy Presidential Library and Museum

Virtue

Jacob Duché Portrait: Public Domain. http://en.wikipedia.org/wiki/File:Jacob_Duche.jpg

Endnotes

[1]*The Rights of the Colonists* by Samuel Adams, 1772

[2]*The Rights of the Colonies Examined* by Stephen Hopkins, Governor of Rhode Island, 1755-1758

About the Authors

Marilyn Boyer is the mother of fourteen children, all home schooled from kindergarten through high school. Her passion to train up her children in the character of Christ led her to create Character Concepts Curriculum, a character curriculum for kids of all ages to equip parents in raising children of integrity!

Her many character resources, as well as books on homeschooling and Christian parenting, are available online.

About the Authors

Grace Tumas Ehrman holds a degree in history from Liberty University. Her paper, "Warlords and Samurais: Japanese Interventionists in Siberia During the Russian Civil War, 1918-1922," won an award at the 2013 Phi Alpha Theta History Conference. She specializes in American and Russian history.

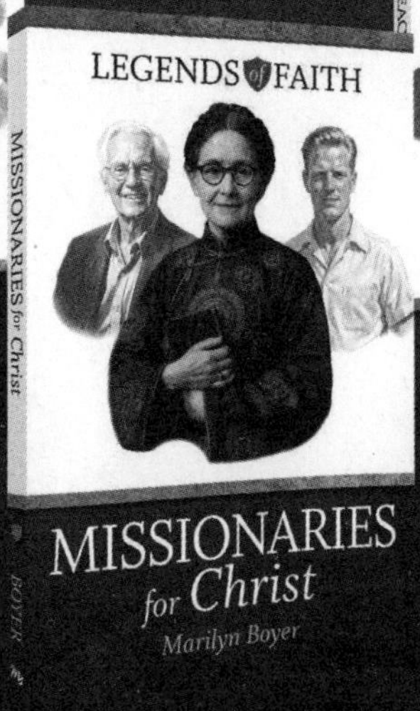